"Unlocking the secrets of Franciscan spirituality, Richard Rohr once again makes the foundational themes of the tradition easily accessible and wonderfully applicable by highlighting their timeliness and perennial qualities in a new way for our time. *Eager to Love* is a gift to all Franciscan-hearted people everywhere!"

—Daniel P. Horan, O.F.M., author, *The Last Words of Jesus: A Meditation on Love and Suffering*

"Richard Rohr is a master weaver, taking the threads of new concepts and understandings and braiding them into a beautiful and profound unified whole. In this new book *Eager to Love*, he illuminates the path of Francis of Assisi as a path of evolving life toward integral wholeness. Weaving thirteenth-century spirituality into the big-bang cosmos, Fr. Rohr brings the Franciscan way of life to the cutting edge of an unfolding universe. This new book reflects his spiritual genius. It should be read by everyone who is seeking to live a radical Christian life."

—Ilia Delio, O.S.F., author, *Compassion: Living in the Spirit of St. Francis*

"I find Richard Rohr one of the most authentic voices for our Christian and perennial wisdom which is rising up today in a common chorus, breaking out of dualism and helping us to hear what will bring us to peace, what is central to all cultures....

"Indeed, this book is vigorously contemplative; a marketplace model of mountaintop living as well as a mountain reflection that asks for day-to-day practice. Wisdom sings out as one cracks the cover of this book, lending to our delight and inviting us to dance the Gospel into the world....

"Rohr is calling us to a sense of light that Francis came to know in his own dark time, thus pointing to Francis and his friend and sister Clare as mentors of light and life. Here he unmasks why wisdom is perennial, present to us in our pain we contemplatively consider and come to a compassionate place in a dark world full of light. Rohr's delight and wry humor helps us go there through his contrasting the Gospel and world today."

—Fr. Dan Riley, O.F.M., founding member,
Mt. Irenaeus Franciscan Mountain Retreat

EAGER TO LOVE

Eager to Love

The Alternative Way of
FRANCIS OF ASSISI

• • •

Richard Rohr

Franciscan
MEDIA
Cincinnati, Ohio

Scripture quotes are from the author's own translation.

Cover and book design by Mark Sullivan
Cover image © Veer | Jarih

LIBRARY OF CONGRESS CATALOGING-IN-PUBLICATION DATA
Rohr, Richard.
Eager to love : the alternative way of Francis of Assisi / Richard Rohr.
pages cm
Includes bibliographical references.
ISBN 978-1-61636-701-5 (alk. paper)
1. Francis, of Assisi, Saint, 1182-1226. 2. Spiritual life—Catholic Church.
3. Christian life—Catholic authors. I. Title.
BX4700.F6R6235 2014
271'.302—dc23
2014016001

ISBN 978-1-61636-701-5

Published by Franciscan Media
28 W. Liberty St.
Cincinnati, OH 45202
www.FranciscanMedia.org

Printed in the United States of America.
Printed on recycled paper.
14 15 16 17 18 5 4 3 2

To several dear ones, who have always been eager to love and sometimes taught me to do the same:

My beloved editor, Sheryl Fullerton, who makes my haphazard way of writing at least somewhat palatable, and sometimes even good.

The three canines in my life—Peanut Butter, the miniature poodle; Gubbio, the Alaskan husky; Venus, my present and beloved black Labrador—who every day in every way have always been "eager to love." (The only people who can say that dogs do not have souls are those who do not know what a soul is or who have never been loved by a dog!)

CONTENTS

:

And so the cycle goes, bringing heavenly Light down and into earthly Life, and then returning Life to Light—thus uniting downward Agape and upward Eros, Descending and Ascending, Compassion and Wisdom, with every breath that you take.[1]

—Ken Wilber

:

Something Old and Something New

Yearning for a new way will not produce it. Only ending the
old way can do that.

You cannot hold onto the old, all the while declaring that you
want something new.

The old will defy the new;

The old will deny the new;

The old will decry the new.

There is only one way to bring in the new. You must make
room for it.[1]

—NEALE DONALD WALSCH

FRANCIS OF ASSISI WAS A master of making room for the new and
letting go of that which was tired or empty. As his first biographer said,
"He was always new, always fresh, always beginning again."[2] Much of
Francis's genius was that he was ready for absolute "newness" from God,

and therefore could also trust fresh and new attitudes in himself. His God was not tired, and so he was never tired. His God was not old, so Francis remained forever young.

There are always new vocabularies, fresh symbols, new frames and styles, but Francis must have known, at least intuitively, that there is only one enduring spiritual insight and everything else follows from it: *The visible world is an active doorway to the invisible world, and the invisible world is much larger than the visible.* I would call this mystical insight "the mystery of incarnation," or the essential union of the material and the spiritual worlds, or simply "Christ."[3]

Our outer world and its inner significance must come together for there to be any wholeness—and holiness. The result is both deep joy and a resounding sense of coherent beauty. What was personified in the body of Jesus was a manifestation of this one universal truth: Matter is, and has always been, the hiding place for Spirit, forever offering itself to be discovered anew. Perhaps this is exactly what Jesus means when he says, "I am the gate" (John 10:7). Francis and his female companion, Clare, carried this mystery to its full and lovely conclusions. Or, more rightly, they were fully carried by it. They somehow knew that the beyond was not really beyond, but in the depths of *here*.

In this book, I want to share with you one of the most attractive, appealing, and accessible of all frames and doorways to the divine.

It is called the *Franciscan way* after the man who first exemplified it, Francesco de Bernardone, who lived in Assisi, Italy, from 1182–1226. Unlike most books on St. Francis and his teachings, I will not begin this book with the usual biographical data, or what is too often jokingly called "birdbath Franciscanism." It is sweet and even consoling, a good enticement, but in the end, harmless and often unreal. Most of us already know the basic story line of his life, and he already has the longest single entry of any one person in the Library of Congress. You can find many good biographies on your own.

A supreme irony I want to mention right at the beginning is that Francis and Clare, two dropouts who totally spurned the entire success, war, and economic agendas of thirteenth-century Assisi, have now been fully sustaining its economy for eight hundred years through the pilgrims and tourists who pour into this lovely medieval town! For centuries now, the Bernardone and Offreduccio families have been very proud of their children—but they surely were not when those children were alive. Francesco and Chiara later became *Saint* Francis and *Saint* Clare, for good but also for ill. As Dorothy Day said about official saints, it allows us to "dismiss them too easily." If we settle for any pretty birdbath Franciscanism, it is very hard to ever get beyond it, nor is it justified in its own social reality.

Francis often functions as an idealized, free, and happy self for many spiritual seekers—from hippies to pious conservatives to socialists to liberal activists—but that is not always the real Francis. Of course, this book will offer quotes and vignettes from Francis's life, but we will mostly be focusing on his lasting meaning, its aftereffects, his legacy itself—down to Pope Francis in our own time—rather than on the romance of his life and our own projections and fantasies about it.

We will first of all examine the ongoing effects and utter newness that emerged after Francis, and then perhaps we will appreciate his revolutionary life with even greater awe. As Søren Kierkegaard said, "We live life forward, but we understand it backward." We will try to do just that with both Francis and Clare. Looking at the many connections that Francis made in his life and that have endured will dramatize how he helped us turn back onto that original but long lost street called the Gospel. We will try to understand Francis by reading his life from what has emerged through his and Clare's imitators and followers who discovered and rediscovered what can only be called *radical simplification*. Here I am thinking of people like Thérèse of Lisieux, Charles de Foucauld, Dorothy Day, Seraphim of Sarov, Nicholas von Flüe, thousands of Catholic and Protestant missionaries, Mother Teresa, and, most recently, Pope Francis. The way of Francis of Assisi cannot be contained inside of formal Franciscanism, simply because it is nothing more than the Gospel itself—in very distilled and honest form.

I want to illustrate here what Francis clearly changed and did differently, and what flowed from his unique wholeness. We will see that Francis was at once very traditional and entirely new in the ways of holiness, and he is still such a standing paradox. He stood barefoot on the earth and yet touched the heavens. He was grounded in the Church and yet instinctively moved toward the cosmos. He lived happily inside the visible and yet both suffered and rejoiced in what others thought was invisible. Again and again, he was totally at home in two worlds at the same time, and thus he made them into one world.

He, like all saints, delighted in both his Absolute Littleness and his Absolute Connection in the very same moment. Of course, they totally depend on one another. He and Clare *died into the life that they loved* instead of living in fear of any death that could end their life. They were both so very eager to love, and they somehow knew that dying to the old and unneeded was an essential part of living this love at any depth. Most of us do not seem to know that—and resist all change.

Yet Francis's holiness, like all holiness, was unique and never a copy or mere imitation. In his "Testament," he says, "No one told me what I ought to do," and then, at the very end of his life, he says, "I have done what was mine to do, now you must do yours." What permission, freedom, and space he thus gave to his followers! Bonaventure echoed that understanding of unique and intimate vocation when he taught,

"We are each loved by God in a particular and incomparable way, as in the case of a bride and bridegroom."[4] Francis and Clare knew that the love God has for each soul is unique and made to order, which is why any "saved" person always feels beloved, chosen, and even "God's favorite" like so many in the Bible. Divine intimacy is always and precisely particular and made to order—and thus "intimate."

Have you noticed that Francis of Assisi is hardly ever pictured with a book, like so many of the teacher saints? Or holding a church building as great churchmen are often painted, or even with his Rule, as Benedict or Basil might be? He is usually pictured glowing, or dancing, in ecstasy, with animals, or with his arms raised to the sky. His liberated body—in touch with everything—is itself his primary message. I have even noted that many paintings of him do not have a halo, as do most holy icons. He is so clearly transformed that we do not need to be reassured that he is among the holy ones, it seems. (If you doubt me, check it out for yourself in art museums!) Francis's body, life, and message seem to glow on their own. A certain radiance and happiness accompanies his very name—Francesco, Franz, François, Francisco, little brother Francis.

Jesus himself, Paul, his iconoclastic interpreter, and both Francis and Clare made room for the new by a full willingness to let go of the old. This is a quite rare pattern in the history of formal religion, which is too often a love affair with small and comfortable traditions. Each of these game-changing people had the courage and the clarity to *sort out* what was perennial wisdom from what was unreal, passing, merely cultural, or even destructive, which is exactly how Jesus describes the way "a disciple of the kingdom" behaves. He says that such disciples are "householders who bring out from their household things both old and new" (Matthew 13:52). John the Baptist describes Jesus as a "winnowing fan" within religion itself—that separates the grain from the chaff (Matthew 3:12)—instead of just presuming that religion is all "grain" and the outsiders are all "chaff."

True spiritual discernment is never as simple as the ego would like to make it. Discernment guides us in doing solid soul work, work that Francis and Clare took on with determination and honesty— with almost no initial counselors, ecclesiastical validation, or outside encouragement. Think about that. Yet they slowly and fully earned the trust and admiration of their contemporaries, even though they were formally breaking most of the cultural and even ecclesiastical rules. (We have no record of either of their fathers ever relenting in their opposition to them, however.)

Franciscanism, however, is not an iconoclastic dismissal of traditional Christian images, history, or culture, but *a positive choosing of the deep, shining, and enduring divine images that are hidden beneath the too-easy formulas.* Theirs is no fast-food religion, but slow and healthy nutrition.

Both Jesus and Francis did not let the old get in the way of the new, but like all religious geniuses, revealed what the old was saying all along. I find much wisdom in what the contemporary faith seeker Christian Wiman writes, but never more than when he says, "Faith itself sometimes needs to be stripped of its social and historical encrustations and returned to its first, churchless incarnation in the human heart."[5]

Francis both named and exemplified that first churchless incarnation of faith in the human heart, but then he somehow also knew that it was the *half-knowing organized Church* that passed this shared mystery on to him and preserved it for future generations. He had the humility and patience to know that whatever is true is always a shared truth, and only institutions, for all their weaknesses, make this widely shareable, historical, and communal. He understood the humility (*kenosis*) and the patience of incarnation. Even a little bit of the truth is more than enough for a saint.

Precisely because both Jesus and Francis were "conservatives," in the true sense of the term, they conserved what was worth conserving— the core, the transformative life of the Gospel—and did not let accidentals get in the way, which are the very things false conservatives usually idolize. They then ended up looking quite "progressive," radical, and even dangerous to the status quo. This is, of course, the constant and consistent biblical pattern, from Abraham to Moses, to Jeremiah, to Job, to John the Baptist, to Mary and Joseph. With courage and wisdom great seers invariably end up saying something exactly like Jesus did: "The law says, and I also say..." (Matthew 5:20–48).

Francis even says to a cardinal who was overseeing an early gathering of the friars, "I do not want to hear any mention of the rule of St. Augustine, of St. Bernard, or of St. Benedict. The Lord has told me that he wanted to make a new fool of me."[6] Wow! That is a mouthful on several levels! Was he rejecting earlier great saints, or was he, in fact, quite sure of what he uniquely had to do, even if it made him look like an idiot, which was a word he once used about himself? Great saints are both courageous and creative; they are "yes, and" or non-dual thinkers who never get trapped in the small world of "either-or" except in the ways of love and courage, where they are indeed *all or nothing*.

The biblical prophets, by definition, were *seers and seekers of Eternal Mystery*, which always seems dangerously new and heretical to old eyes and any current preoccupations with security. The prophets lived *on the edge of the inside* of Judaism. John the Baptist later does the same with Temple Judaism, and Paul then sharply disagrees with Peter and the new Christian establishment in Jerusalem (Galatians 2:1–14). Francis and Clare continued this classic pattern in their own hometown as they physically moved from upper Assisi among the *majores* to the lower side of town and the *minores*.[7]

EAGER TO LOVE :

There they had nothing to prove or defend, plus the most opportunities to have fresh and honest experience—and to find their True Center. It is ironic that you must go to the edge to find the center. But that is what the prophets, hermits, and mystics invariably know. Only there were they able to live at the edges of their own lives too, not grasping at the superficial or protecting the surfaces of things, but falling into the core and center of their own souls and their own experiences.

You can now let Francis and Clare show you how to die into your one and only life, the life that you must learn to love. It will show itself to be one continuous movement—first learning to love your life and then allowing yourself to fully *die into it*—and never to die away from it. Once death is joyfully incorporated into life, you are already in heaven, and there is no possibility or fear of hell. That is the Franciscan way. *The Gospel is not a fire insurance policy for the next world, but a life assurance policy for this world.* Francis and Clare somehow came to see through the common disguises of heaven and hell,[8] and they seemed to come to this on their own somehow! My hope and desire in writing this book is that you can know heaven on your own too, and *now*!

CHAPTER ONE

What Do We Mean by "Mysticism"?

As with lovers,

When it's right, you can't say

Who is kissing whom.[1]

—GREGORY ORR

THE MOST UNFORTUNATE THING ABOUT the concept of mysticism is that the word itself has become *mystified*—and relegated to a "misty" and distant realm that implies it is only available to a very few. For me, the word simply means *experiential knowledge of spiritual things*, as opposed to book knowledge, secondhand knowledge or even church knowledge.[2]

Most of organized religion, without meaning to, has actually discouraged us from taking the mystical path by telling us almost exclusively to trust outer authority, Scripture, tradition, or various kinds of experts (what I call the "containers")—instead of telling us the value and importance of inner experience itself (which is the "content"). In fact, most of us were strongly warned against *ever* trusting ourselves. Roman Catholics were told to trust the church hierarchy first and last, while mainline Protestants were often warned that inner experience was dangerous, unscriptural, or even unnecessary.

Both were ways of discouraging actual experience of God and often created passive (and often passive aggressive) people and, more sadly, a lot of people who concluded that there was no God to be experienced. We were taught to mistrust our own souls—and thus the Holy Spirit! Contrast that with Jesus's common phrase, "Go in peace, your faith has made you whole!" He said this to people who had made no dogmatic affirmations, did not think he was "God," did not pass any moral check-list, and often did not belong to the "correct" group! *They were simply people who trustfully affirmed, with open hearts, the grace of their own hungry experience—in that moment—and that God could care about it!*

Pentecostals and charismatics are a significant modern-era exception to this avoidance of experience, and I believe their "baptism in the Spirit" is a true and valid example of initial mystical encounter. The only things they lack, which often keep them from mature mysticism, are solid theology, some developmental psychology, and some social concerns to keep their feet in this incarnate world. Without these, their authentic but ego-inflating experience has often led to superficial and conservative theology and even right-wing politics. But the core value and truth of experience is still there, right beneath the surface.[3]

The irony in all of these attempts to over-rely on externals is that people end up relying upon their own experience anyway! We all—by necessity—see everything through the lens of our own temperament, early conditioning, brain function, role and place in society, education, our personal needs, and our unique cultural biases and assumptions. Yes, our experiences are indeed easy to misinterpret, as we universalize from our "moment" to an expectation that everybody must have the same kind of "moment." That only gives us the excuse to mistrust such narcissism in people even more. Or, more commonly, people assume that their experience is 100 percent from God with no filters developed that would clear away their own agenda and their own ego. They forget Paul's reminder which was meant to keep us humble: "We know imperfectly and we prophesy imperfectly" (1 Corinthians 13:9).

To help us escape from this trap, the formerly rare ministry of spiritual direction is being rediscovered and revalued in our time, especially among the laity. It is a proven way to hold personal experience accountable to Scripture, common sense, reason, frankly some good psychology, and the Tradition (I use uppercase-T Tradition to refer to the constantly recurring "Perennial Tradition," and lowercase-t tradition to refer to the common "we have always done it this way"). All together this might be the best way to hear and trust "God's will." We have much to thank the Jesuits for in this regard, although there are now other excellent schools of spiritual direction available too.

I think you will find that Franciscan mysticism, in particular, is a trustworthy and simple—though not necessarily easy—path precisely because it refuses to be mystified by doctrinal abstractions, moralism, or false asceticism (although some Franciscans have gone this route). Franciscanism is truly a *sidewalk spirituality* for the streets of the world, a path highly possible and attractive for all would-be seekers. You don't need to be celibate, isolated from others, more highly educated, or in any way superior to your neighbor—as many Secular Franciscans have shown us. In fact, those kinds of paths might well get in the way of the experience itself. A celibate hermit can have a totally dualistic mind[4] and live a tortured inner life—and thus torture others too. A busy jour-nalist or housewife with a non-dual heart and mind can enlighten other individuals, their family, and all they touch, without talking "religiously" at all. Think Nelson Mandela, Mary Oliver, or Wendell Berry.

I will try to summarize the Franciscan mystical path to the Divine in specific ways here, and I will distinguish them from other paths so you can better appreciate the uniqueness of Francis's genius. He cut to the essentials and avoided what had been, and continues to be, a preoccupation with nonessentials. Even Thomas Aquinas said that the actual precepts Jesus taught were "very few." Each of the possible diversions I will name must have been a "temptation to him," just as they were to the young Buddha. In the Franciscan worldview, separation from the world is the monastic temptation, asceticism is the temptation of the desert fathers and mothers, moralism or celibacy is the Catholic temptation, intellectualizing is the seminary temptation, privatized piety and inerrant belief is the Protestant temptation, and the most common temptation for all of us is to use *belonging to the right group and practicing its proper rituals* as a substitute for any personal or life-changing encounter with the Divine.

How Francis managed to avoid all of these common temptations, and also steer through them, is at the heart of his spiritual genius. Further, he was able to do all of this while also belonging to groups that he loved. He knew that some kind of base camp is the only testing ground for actual faith, hope, or charity. We need living communities to keep us accountable, growing, and honest. Francis was not a modern individualist.

I don't know that we Franciscans have always followed him very well in avoiding these temptations. And, of course, not everyone in these groups I've just mentioned surrendered to these temptations. I point out these diversionary paths to help us clarify the essential issue, and not to criticize anyone—monks, Protestants, or academics. These characterizations help us see how Francis eventually maneuvered his way through all of these nonessentials, largely by intuition and the Holy Spirit. Much of his genius was that he did this by trusting his own inner experience, the very thing Catholics were normally discouraged from doing. Remember what he said in his "Testament": "There was no one to tell me what I should do."[5]

The Infinite in the Finite

Francis knew that if you can accept that the finite manifests the infinite, and that the physical is the doorway to the spiritual (which is the foundational principle we call "incarnation"), then all you need is right here and right now—in this world. *This* is the way to *that!* Heaven includes earth. Time opens you up to the timeless, space opens you up to space-lessness, if you only take them for the clear doorways that they are. There are not sacred and profane things, places, and moments. There are only sacred and *desecrated* things, places, and moments—and it is *we alone* who desecrate them by our blindness and lack of reverence. It is one sacred universe, and we are all a part of it. You really cannot get any better or more simple than that, in terms of a spiritual vision.

The realization that the concrete opens you up to the universal might be the only fully trustworthy or possible path anyway, because that is how sensate humans normally operate. Abstract ideology will not get you very far, and much common religion is ideology more than any real encounter with Presence. But we all must start with our anecdotal experience, and then build from there. What else can we do? Good spiritual teachers tell you *how* to build from there! Wise people, Scripture, and Tradition tell you what of your experience is worth looking at and what is perhaps a detour or a dead end. When religion becomes mere ideology (or even mere theology!), it starts with universal theories and the rubber never hits the road again. As Pope Francis says, people all over the world are rejecting this ideological (top down) form of religion—and they should because this is not the path of Christ himself.

By taking the mystery of the Incarnation absolutely seriously, and gradually extending it to its logical conclusions, the seeming limitations of space and time are once and for all overcome in Francis. The Christ Mystery refuses to be vague or abstract, and is always concrete and specific. When we stay with these daily apparitions, we see that everything is a revelation of the divine—from rocks to rocket ships. There are henceforth no blind spots in the divine disclosure, in our own eyes, or in our rearview mirrors. Our only blindness is our own lack of fascination, humility, curiosity, awe, and willingness to be allured forward.[6]

WHAT YOU SEE IS WHAT YOU ARE
Franciscan spirituality emphasizes a real equivalence and mutuality between the one who sees and what can be seen. There is a symbiosis

between the mind and heart of the seer—and to what they will then pay attention. Francis had a unique ability to call others—animals, planets and elements—"brother" and "sister" because he himself was a little brother. He granted other beings and things mutuality, subjectivity, "personhood," and dignity because he first honored his own dignity as a son of God. (Although it could be the other way around too!) The world of things was a transparent two-way mirror for him, which some of us would call a fully "sacramental" universe.[7]

All *being* can correctly and rightly be spoken of with "one voice" (*univocity*), as John Duns Scotus will later put it (see chapter thirteen). What I am you also are, and so is the world. *Creation is one giant symphony of mutual sympathy.* Or, as Augustine loved to say, "In the end there will only be Christ loving himself."

To get to this 3-D vision, *I must know that I am, at least in part, the very thing I am seeking. In fact that is what makes me seek it!*[8] But most do not know this good news yet. God cannot be found "out there" until God is first found "in here," within ourselves, as Augustine had profoundly expressed in his *Confessions* in many ways. Then we can almost naturally see God in others and in all of creation too. *What you seek is what you are.* The search for God and the search for our True Self are finally the same search.[9] Francis's all-night prayer, "Who are you, O

God, and who am I?" is probably a perfect prayer, because it is the most honest prayer we can offer.

REMAIN IN LOVE

A heart transformed by this realization of oneness knows that only love "in here" can spot and enjoy love "out there." Fear, constriction, and resentment are seen by spiritual teachers to be an inherent blindness that must be overcome. Those emotions cannot get you anywhere, certainly not anywhere good. Thus all mystics are positive people—or they are not mystics! Their spiritual warfare is precisely the work of recognizing and then handing over *all* of their inner negativity and fear to God. The great paradox here is that such a victory is a total gift from God and yet somehow you must want it very much (Philippians 2:12–13).

The central practice in Franciscan mysticism, therefore, is that we *must remain in love*, which is why it is a commandment as such (John 15:9), in fact, *the* commandment of Jesus. Only when we are *eager to love* can we see love and goodness in the world around us. We must ourselves remain in peace, and then we will see and find peace over there. Remain in beauty, and we will honor beauty everywhere. This concept of *remaining* or *abiding* (John 15:4–5) moves all religion out of any esoteric realms of doctrinal outer space where it has for too long been lost. There is no secret moral command for knowing or pleasing

God, or what some call "salvation," beyond becoming a loving person in mind, heart, body, and soul yourself. Then you will see what you need to see. This teaching is so central that we made it the title of this book: we all must be very eager to love—every day.

ONE SACRED WORLD

In Franciscan mysticism, there is no distinction between sacred and profane. All of the world is sacred, as I said previously. In other words, you can pray always, and everything that happens is potentially sacred if you allow it to be. Our job as humans is to make admiration of others and adoration of God fully conscious and deliberate. It is the very purpose of life. As the French friar Eloi Leclerc beautifully put into the mouth of Francis, "If we but knew how to adore, we could travel through the world with the tranquility of the great rivers."[10]

For those who have learned how to see—and adore—everything is "spiritual," which ironically and eventually leads to what Dietrich Bonhoeffer courageously called "religionless Christianity." (Don't be scared by that!) By that he meant many people, even in his time of the 1930s, were moving beyond the scaffolding of religion to the underlying and deeper Christian experience itself. Once we can accept that God is in all situations, and can and will use even bad situations for good, then everything becomes an occasion for good and an occasion for God, and is thus at the heart of religion. The Center is everywhere.

God's plan is so perfect that even sin, tragedy, and painful deaths are used to bring us to divine union. *God wisely makes the problem itself part of the solution.* It is all a matter of learning how to see rightly, fully, and therefore truthfully. Recently, I watched a family-made video of a dear teenage daughter's last moments dying from cancer, as she lovingly said good-bye to them, and the family was ecstatic with tears and joy, through profound faith in eternal life and love. Such a fully human love is probably going to do more long-lasting good for that family than years of formal religious education. I know that to be true from many personal experiences. That is "religionless Christianity," which ironically might be the most religious of all.

Paradoxes at the Edges

Franciscan spirituality boldly puts a big exclamation point behind Jesus's words that "The last will be first and the first will be last!" and Paul's "When I am weak I am strong!" *Upside-downness* is at the heart of our message, always prompting us to look more deeply and broadly. This opens up our eyes to recognize God's self-giving at the far edges where most of us cannot or will not see God, such as other religions, any who are defined as outsider or sinner, and even to the far edge of our seeing, toward those who are against us—our so-called enemies. In fact, truth, love, and beauty are most beautifully found at the lowest, weakest, and most concrete possible levels, like in a frog, a fugitive, or what others might call a freak. You have to accept God's divine freedom to see this way! You must grow up to your full stature to find the full stature of God (Ephesians 4:13). Small souls are incapable of knowing a great God, and great souls are never satisfied with a small or stingy God. You have to become conscious yourself, and then all things will be beautiful.

Seeming absence, ironically, becomes the deepest recognition of presence, because it is thus awaited and needed. The entire world is indeed sacramental and mediates the message, and yet it is hidden in such a way that only the humble and honest—and suffering—will find it. Bonaventure said that an uneducated washer woman could, without even knowing it, be much closer to God than a doctor in theology such as himself.

Francis's own intuitive wisdom did not come from the outside or the top, but from deep inside him, because he allowed his heart to be broken and poor, especially when his vision for the friars was largely abandoned in his own lifetime. It is there that God can most loudly speak—which is really a constant Biblical theme,[11] reaching its apogee in Jesus's inaugural line "How blessed are the poor in spirit" (Matthew 5:3).

Note also how Francis was able to trust his own limited, formally uneducated, and simple human experience to know what he then knew with such calm conviction. Very early on, for example, when the friars were already being invited to dine with bishops and serve as court chaplains to cardinals, he strongly speaks against accepting these gracious invitations and says "You are thus being drawn away from the womb of your mother."[12] Now if he really said this, he is either anti-social, holier than thou, or he quietly knows what his core God experience demands. There is no secondhand knowledge of God for Francis and Clare. The best window to knowledge is through "the crack in everything,"[13] as Leonard Cohen puts it. Francis wanted us to stay close to the cracks in the social fabric, and not to ensconce ourselves at the safe, even churchy, center. Not only were we Franciscans not to be prelates in the church, but we should not hobnob there too much. You tend to think like those with whom you party.

My God and All Things

Finally, any temptation to either elitism or individualism is strongly overcome in Franciscan mysticism by its adamant insistence on identification with the cross, solidarity with the poor, and with human suffering in general. Solidarity with the suffering of the world and *even with the suffering of God* is Francis's starting place, and not any kind of search for private moral perfection. This keeps the contemplative journey from mere introversion, sweet piety, private salvation, or any antisocial or privatized message, whereby I imagine that I can come to

God by myself apart from union with everything else. The Franciscan motto is thus *Deus Meus et Omnia*, "My God—and *all things.*"

Francis had to be so adamant about the poor and poverty because he knew that *"spirituality," in itself and apart from others, without service and concrete love, often leads people to immense ego inflation and delusion.* Wanting to be thought holy, special, right, safe, or on higher moral ground has a deep narcissistic appeal to the human ego. These false motivations are, ironically, the surest ways to actually avoid God—all the while using much God talk and ritualized behavior.

The great irony of faith is that authentic God experience does indeed make you know you are quite special, favorite, and chosen—but you realize others are too! That is the giveaway that your experience is authentic, although it might take a while to get there. You are indeed hurting—and others are too. Your only greatness is that you share the common greatness of the whole communion of saints. Your membership in the communion of sinners is a burden you can now carry patiently because others are also carrying it with you. You are finally inside of what Thomas Merton calls "the general dance." You no longer need to be personally correct as much as you just need to be *connected.*

A Mysticism for Daily Life

So Franciscan mysticism is indeed mysticism, but it is especially poised and prepared to lead people not just to inner experience, but to the possibility of daily and regular experience in the depth and beauty of the ordinary, especially because it incorporates the seeming negative and moves our life to its hard edges, thus making things like failure, tragedy, and suffering the quickest doorways to the encounter of God. All can now enter if they are honest about their poverty.

There is nothing that God cannot and will not use to bring us to divine union—even sin (*felix culpa*). That is the full glory, effectiveness, and universality of the Gospel in its simple and clear splendor. In short, Francis democratizes the whole spiritual journey, and lets us know that it is available outside of monasteries, celibacy, moralism, or false asceticism, which has not always been obvious in most Christian (or non-Christian!) spiritualities. This is surely why G.K. Chesterton called Francis "the world's one quite sincere democrat."[14]

If Christ is the first idea in the mind of God, as John Duns Scotus teaches, if the Christ Mystery is revealed already in the Big Bang, then *grace is inherent to creation from the beginning* and not a later add-on, or a dole-out to the worthy or the churched, or a prize for the perfect. This completely rearranges the spiritual universe most of us were educated into, where grace was an add-on, an occasional filling of the gaps, a churchy thing, a prize for the perfect, and, even then, only now and then.

Did you ever notice in the Gospels that, even after two appearances of the Risen Christ, the Apostles return to their old job of fishing (John 21:3)? They don't join the priesthood, try to get a job at the Temple, go on more retreats, take vows, leave their wives, get a special title, nor is there any mention of them even getting baptized, or wearing special clothing beyond that of a wayfarer or "workman" (Matthew 10:9–10). When the inner is utterly transformed, you do not need symbolic outer validations, special hats, or flashy insignia (although I do like the pallium the pope and archbishops wear, which must be made of lamb's wool and worn over their shoulders, to remind them that they must always be willing to carry the weak lambs).

Note also that the Risen Christ himself is not ever apparent as a supernatural figure, but mistaken in one case for a gardener, another time for a fellow traveler on the road, and then for a fisherman offering advice. *He seems to look just like everybody else after the Resurrection* (John 20:15; Luke 24:13–35; John 21:4), even with his wounds on full display! In the Gospels and in Franciscan spirituality, we can all go back to "fishing" after any authentic God encounter, consciously carrying our humiliating wounds, but now almost like a badge of honor. In fact, it is exactly our woundedness that gives us any interest in healing itself, and the very power to heal others. As Henri Nouwen rightly said, the only authentic healers are always wounded healers. Most good therapists will tell you the same.

True mysticism just allows us to "fish" from a different side of the boat, and with a different expectation of what success might mean, all the while totally assured that we are already floating on a big, deep, and life-filled pond. The mystical heart knows that there is a fellow Fisherman nearby who is always available for good advice. He is standing and beckoning from the shores and at the edges of every ordinary life (John 21:5), every unreligious moment, every "secular" occupation, and he is still talking to working men and women who, like the first disciples, were not important, influential, especially "holy," trained in theology, or even educated. This is the mystical doorway for all things Franciscan, which is not narrow but wide and welcoming.

But let's also name, as Jesus honestly does, a necessary narrowing of that doorway too: Our inherent and common resistance to suffering (Luke 13:2). Yes, it is an open door, but the parameters for walking through it are also clear. Both Jesus and Francis had to make *necessary suffering* clear, because they knew that everything within us would avoid the cross of transformation. It becomes for both of them "the royal road" to understanding spiritual things, and this message utterly levels the playing field of spirituality—because all humans in fact suffer in one way or another. That we have in common. So let's go there now.

CHAPTER TWO

A Happy Run Downward:
The Inner Authority of Those Who Have Suffered

Might the authority of those who suffer bring the diverse
cultural and social worlds together?[1]

—JOHANN BAPTIST METZ

I BELIEVE THIS PROFOUND QUESTION about suffering from a modern
German theologian succinctly and precisely expresses the religious
breakthrough that Christ has offered humanity. It is also foundational
to understanding the unique Franciscan view of the world. True gospel
authority, the authority to heal and renew things and people, is not
finally found in a hierarchical office, a theological argument, a perfect
law, or a rational explanation. What the crucified has revealed to the
world is that the real authority that "authors" people[2] and changes the
world *is an inner authority that comes from people who have lost, let go, and
are refound on a new level.* Twelve-step programs have come to much
the same conclusion in our time.

A Happy Run Downward

I present this mystery close to the beginning of the book because I believe both Francis and Clare had this kind of inner authority, and it is still part of their essential message for the world. They lost and let go of all fear of suffering; all need for power, prestige, and possessions; and all need for their small self to be important, and they came out the other side knowing something essential—who they really were in God and thus who they really were. Their house was then built on "bedrock," as Jesus says (Matthew 7:24).

Such an ability to really change and heal people is often the fruit of suffering, and various forms of poverty, since the false self does not surrender without a fight to its death.[3] If suffering is "whenever we are not in control" (which is my definition), then you see why some form of suffering is absolutely necessary to teach us how to live beyond the illusion of control and to give that control back to God. Then we become usable instruments, because we can share our power with God's power (Romans 8:28).

Such a totally counterintuitive insight surely explains why these two medieval dropouts tried to invite us all into their happy run downward, to that place of "poverty" where all humanity finally dwells anyway. They voluntarily leapt into the very fire from which most of us are trying to escape, with total trust that Jesus's way of the cross could not, and would not, be wrong. They trusted that his way was the way of solidarity and communion with the larger world which is indeed passing away and dying—but always with great resistance. They turned such resistance into a proactive welcoming prayer instead. By God's grace, they could trust the eventual passing of all things, and where it was passing to. They did not wait for liberation later—after death—but grasped it here and now.

When we try to live in solidarity with the pain of the world—and do not spend our lives running from necessary suffering—we will encounter various forms of "crucifixion." Many say pain is physical discomfort, but suffering comes from our resistance, denial, and sense of injustice or wrongness about that pain. I know that is very true for me. This is the core meaning of suffering on one level or another, and we all learn it the hard way. Pain is the rent we pay for being human, it seems, but suffering is usually optional. *The cross was Jesus's voluntary acceptance of undeserved suffering as an act of total solidarity with all of the pain of the world.* Reflection on this mystery of love can change your whole life.

It seems there is an inherent negative energy or resistance from all of us, whenever we are invited to a more generous response. Yet it is the necessary dying that the soul must walk through to go higher, further, deeper, or longer. The saints called these dyings "nights," darkness, or seasons of unknowing and doubt. Our secular world has almost no spiritual skills to deal with this now, so we resort to pills, addictions, and other distractions to get us through. This does not bode well for the future of humanity.

Only truly inspired souls like Francis and Clare voluntarily choose to fully jump on board this ship of life and death. They fully rode the resistance to which the rest of us surrender. Our lives can take this same ride—whenever we try to hold any negativity or self-doubt with integrity, and when we "suffer" the full truth of any situation instead of just taking what we think is the one righteous side. Integrity is often a willingness to hold the dark side of things instead of reacting against them, denying them, or projecting our anxiety elsewhere. Frankly, it is just another name for faith. Without the inner discipline of faith, most lives end in negativity, blaming, or deep cynicism—without even knowing it.

Jesus hung in the crucified middle and paid the price for all such reconciliation with reality in its wounded state (Ephesians 2:13–18); then he invited us to do the same. And Francis did so wholeheartedly! St. Bernadine of Siena attributed this prayer to Francis: "You who have deigned to die for love of my love, let me know the sweet violence of that love; and let me die for love of Your love."[4]

Solidarity with the Larger Pain of the World
I think the acceptance of that invitation to solidarity with the larger

pain of the world is what it means to be "a Christian." It takes great inner freedom to be a follower of Jesus. *His life is an option, a choice, a call, a vocation, and we are totally free to say yes or no or maybe. You do not have to do this to make God love you. That is already taken care of.* You do it to love God back and to love what God loves and how God loves! You either are baptized "into his death" and "resurrection" (Romans 6:3; Philippians 3:10–12), or Christianity is largely a mere belonging system, not a transformational system that will change the world.

The cruciform shape of reality became the very shape of Francis's body in the last two years of his life after he received the stigmata, or the marks of the five wounds of Christ in his body. The baffling and shocking mystery of a person carrying the physical wounds of Jesus— that took psychosomatic shape in Francis's very body—had never been seen before in human history. Bonaventure portrays the *stigmatized* ("marked") Francis coming down the mountain "bearing the representation of Christ crucified reproduced in his own body."[5] He soon became the most painted saint in Christian art. Bonaventure saw him as a new Moses, who instead of bringing tablets of stone down the mountain brought an astounding message of total solidarity with divine and human suffering. With these marks, Francis joined Jesus as "the man of sorrows," and he joyfully lived suffering itself in a way that was redemptive and transformative for the world and for others.[6]

The "crucified God"[7] as personified in Jesus revealed that *God is always on the side of suffering wherever it is found,* including the wounded and dying troops on *both* sides in every kind of war, and both the victims and the predators of this world, which frankly pleases very few people. (Identification with suffering might just be non-dual thinking in its most active and proactive form and why nonviolence demands such a high level of transformation.) Our resistance to suffering is an entire industry now, perhaps symbolized by the total power of the gun lobby and the permanent war economy in America, the fear of any profit sharing with the poor, or the need to be constantly entertained. Maybe that is why some have said that the foundational virtue underlying all others is courage (*"cor-agere"* = an action of the heart). It takes immense courage to walk in solidarity with the suffering of others, and even our own.

Francis seems to have fully embraced the cruciform shape of reality, and maybe that was his great act of courage. As one Dutch Franciscan put it, Francis of Assisi became a living and dying "Covenant with God's poor" and with the universal suffering of humanity,[8] just as Jesus had done. The shocked response to Pope Francis's choice of this name shows how much the world intuitively understands this symbolism. And it was understood even more when, soon after his election, he said, "I want us to be a church that is poor and for the poor."

I have come to believe that Jesus's solidarity with suffering on the cross is actually *an acceptance of a certain meaninglessness in the universe*, its nonsensical tragic nature, a black hole that seems constantly to show itself to sensitive souls. To accept some degree of meaninglessness is our final and full act of faith that God is still good and still in control. How hard that is to do sometimes. The final and full gift of meaning is ironically the incorporation of "no meaning" and not knowing. This is the same mystical mind of faith that emerges in all of the world's religions at the more mature levels, but a "crucified god" places this issue absolutely front and center, so we cannot miss the point and to save us from our common despair.

I was recently struck by the tragic and sad nature of the world when I saw pictures of the tens of thousands of cattle who froze to death from an early spring blizzard in South Dakota, and then the horrible typhoon in the Philippines. "Why?" I said to God. Yet I have to believe that the God who knows when sparrows fall (Matthew 10:29) and says that "not one is forgotten in God's sight" (Luke 12:6) knows and deeply cares that most animals and humans die painful deaths. God's presence first hides—and yet ironically is also revealed—in such seeming total absence, but only for those who search and ask. The "problem of good" shines the brightest after we struggle, and when we patiently struggle, with the more nonsensical "problem of evil."

There is nothing ascetical or morbid here, or any negative message that "you should suffer more." That overreaction misses the earth-shattering proclamation that suffering makes about the very nature of God and all those who love him. Instead, it reveals that to accept *full reality* will always be a kind of crucifixion both for God and for ourselves. For us, it is a sure death to our easy opinions, our forced certitudes, any futile attempts at perfect control, our preplanned life, any intellectual or moral superiority, and eventually any belief in our separateness from God. Jesus on the cross says that God is somehow *in* and *with* all these dyings! This is a trusting that stretches us to our limits many times, just as it did Jesus (Matthew 27:46).

Suffering seems to overcome the semipermeable membrane between ourselves, others, and God—and sometimes rather completely. It can overcome all of the major splits from reality that we all enter into: the split from our shadow self, the split of mind from our body, the split of death from life, and the split into separateness from God and others.[9] Overcoming these foundational splits is what I mean by necessary suffering, and is almost the definition of any in-depth spirituality.

THE PARADOX OF SUFFERING

This acceptance of growth through suffering is what gives us wisdom and spiritual authority, and finally teaches us love itself—as a gift from beyond. *Spiritual authority is first of all inner authority, but then it can become an outer authority too.* Jesus calls this servant leadership (Luke 22:24–27), which is his way of speaking of bottom-up and inside-out authority. Such authority might come from the single mothers, happily working three jobs to support three children, who change our lives much more than the authoritative sermon from the pulpit. These might be the people who can speak *with quiet conviction* in a way that actually and deeply *convicts us.* Such inner authority is absolutely necessary to balance an all-too-common reliance on mere outer authority, which so often creates very passive or very rebellious "believers" in all religions.

The "coincidence of opposites" (the inherent contradictions that almost everything carries) is what crucified Jesus, and it is this world of contradictions to which he said yes. If we hang there with him, *patiently and prayerfully holding the paradoxes of every single thing that lives*, we will henceforth know, teach, live, and believe in a very different way, plus we will enjoy a "peace that the world cannot give" (John 14:27). The Christian code words for this essential mystery— that must always be held together as one—are "death and resurrection of Jesus." But most Christians just *worship* this historical event in Jesus, and profusely thank him for it—instead of setting out on the same path themselves. It is probably the classic example of missing the major point among Christians of all denominations. We worship revelations *out there* instead of also recognizing them *in here*. And the world remains unchanged.

The most obvious change that results from such a holding and allowing is that we will naturally become much more compassionate and much more patient.[10] Compassion and patience are the absolutely unique characteristics of true spiritual authority, and without any doubt are the way both Francis and Clare led their communities. They led not from above, and not even from below, but mostly from *within*, by walking *with* their brothers and sisters, or "smelling like the sheep," as Pope Francis puts it. A spiritual leader who lacks basic human compassion has almost no power to change other people, because people intuitively know he or she does not represent the Divine or Big Truth. Such leaders have to rely upon role, laws, and enforcement powers to effect any change in others. Such change does not go deep, nor does it last. In fact, it is not really change at all.

The Authority of Being "Refound"

People, however, who are led to the edge of their own resources, as Jesus was on the cross, and find themselves at an utterly new level, are what we mean by being "refound" or resurrected. And they can say with Paul, "I live no longer, not I, but Christ lives in me" (Galatians 2:20). Their authority comes from a deeper place and a more convicting place than

"I have the right to say this." It feels more like "I have earned the right to say this," which has a whole different weight and heft.

These are the folks who can heal, reconcile, understand, and change others. Such a basis for authority is universally available, and not in any way the unique province of any one religion, belief system, education, or ordination. It is the authority of having been in *the place of no control over the outcome*, and then coming out the other side—larger and more alive, and thus able to invite others into that same and Bigger Field. Francis and Clare are examples of people who dive into this Bigger Field of paradox and absurdity with complete freedom and choice—*beforehand*—and then the *during* and the *after* somehow take care of themselves! Faith does a "preemptive strike" at both life and death, which makes the rest of the journey of every saint a happy "See, I told you so!"

The pattern for this new kind of authority was taught by Jesus when he said, "Simon, you must be sifted like wheat and I will pray that you will not fail; and *once you have recovered*, you in your turn can strengthen the brothers [and sisters]" (Luke 22:31–32). This *sifting and then recovering* is Peter's real and life-changing authority, as it is for anybody. Unless a bishop, teacher, or minister has on some level walked through suffering, failure, or humiliation, his or her words will tend to be fine but superficial, OK but harmless, heard by the ears but unable to touch the soul. It is interesting to me that twelve-step programs have come to be called the "Recovery" movement. They are onto something!

Once we go through our own sifting—and recovering—we will have a kind of real inner authority too, by just trusting what we know. It will probably never be an authority that needs to be formally licensed as such, just as Francis and Clare sought no church office or ordination, but instead expresses an inherent authority to heal and change situations and people—just like the janitor at school with whom the students share their problems or the single and poor mother who has raised four children and is still in love with life.

Such is the final tour de force that the Gospel offers to the institutions of this world, as they clamor for what is too often false authority. I am afraid you can easily be ordained a minister in most churches largely by passing tests, and formal ministry can be a mere career move "upward" which might be an attempt to avoid all moving "downward"—as if we could. Do not be shocked, but I suspect some priests' and ministers' moral failures are actually very helpful to their own "salvation" and necessary for their growing up. I have counseled many of them. Francis knew this truth—it is why he did not at first want his Order to be priests at all—but if so, a very different kind of priest who identified with the poor and the weak and, most especially, their own poverty. He wanted our authority to be built on bedrock and not on sand.

Our Christ "reigns" from the cross, but with a new kind of power that looks and feels like total weakness, just as all human suffering and humiliation does. Only those who have joined him there and come out the other side, like Francis and his authentic followers, will understand this. They "rule" from the edges and reign from what is no longer the bottom.

CHAPTER THREE

Living on the Edge of the Inside:
Simplicity and Justice

My brothers, my brothers, God has called me to walk in the
way of humility, and showed me the way of simplicity.... The
Lord has shown me that he wants me to be a new kind of
fool in the world, and God does not want to lead us by any
other knowledge than that.[1]

—FRANCIS OF ASSISI

FRANCIS AND CLARE WERE NOT so much prophets by what they said
as in the radical, system-critiquing way that they lived their lives. They
found both their inner and outer freedom by structurally living *on
the edge of the inside of both church and society*. Too often people seek
either inner freedom or outer freedom, but seldom—very seldom in my
opinion—do people find both. They did.

Francis and Clare's agenda for justice was the most foundational and
undercutting of all others: a very simple lifestyle outside the system of

production and consumption (the real meaning of the vow of poverty), plus a conscious identification with the marginalized of society (the communion of saints pushed to its outer edge). In this position you do not "do" acts of peace and justice as much as your life is *itself* peace and justice. You take your small and sufficient place in the great and grand scheme of God. By "living on the edge of the inside" I mean building on the solid Tradition ("from the inside") but doing it from a new and creative stance where you cannot be coopted for purposes of security, possessions, or the illusions of power ("on the edge").

It is worth repeating that Francis and Clare placed themselves outside the system of not just *social* production and consumption, but ecclesiastical too! Remember, Francis was not a priest, nor were Franciscan men originally or primarily priests. Theirs was not a spirituality of earning, or any seeking of worthiness, career, church status, moral one-upmanship, or divine favor (which they knew they already had). They represented in their own unique way the old tradition of "holy fools" among the desert fathers and mothers and the Eastern Church, and offered that notion to the very organized and "efficient" Western Church. For the most part, the path they offered has been ignored or not understood, just as restorative justice usually is. Most prefer *quid pro quo* justice (retributive justice), which is the best that most secular systems can offer. But those formed by the Gospels should know better.

A SIMPLE WAY OF LIFE

This simple way of life on the edge of the inside offered a radically different perspective about the meaning of church itself. The holding of church offices and public church roles came later for the friars. (But not for Franciscan sisters. Should we say "Thank God!"?) These two dropouts from thirteenth-century Assisi society found a place of structural freedom, and then inside of that also found personal, mental, and emotional freedom, although I am not sure which came first. To be both outside of these social and ecclesiastical systems, and free from negativity and ego within ourselves, could well be a definition of full gospel freedom, and at the core of the biblical tradition of "the poor of Yahweh" or the *anawim*.[2] This was again strongly rediscovered in the twentieth century in many liberation theologians and their "preferential option for the poor."

Today, most of us try to find personal and individual freedom even as we remain inside of structural boxes and an entire system of consumption that we are then unable or unwilling to critique. Our mortgages, luxuries, and chosen lifestyles control our whole future. Whoever is paying our bills, and giving us security and status, determines what we can and cannot say, or even what we can or cannot think. You cannot remove the plank that you are standing on. Self-serving institutions that give us our security, status, or identity are almost always considered "too big to fail" and are invariably beyond any honest critique for the vast majority of people.[3] And thus corruption grows. *The way of radical Christianity is simply to stay outside of such systems to begin with, so they cannot control your breadth of thinking, feeling, loving, and living out universal justice.*

Only some contemporary prophets, like Dorothy Day, have had the courage to name the world as "a dirty rotten system." (I would be afraid to say that myself because it might sound negative or angry.) When Jesus and John's Gospel used the term "the world," they did not mean the earth, creation, or civilization, which Jesus clearly came to love and save (John 12:47). They were referring to *idolatrous systems and institutions that are invariably self-referential and always passing away* (1 Corinthians 7:31). It is very similar to the way Buddhists speak of all things as "empty."

This "dirty rotten system" that Dorothy dismisses is the very one Francis and Clare avoided. When Francis said, after kissing the leper, "I left the world,"[4] he was saying that he was giving up on *the usual payoffs, constraints, and rewards of business-as-usual* and was choosing to live in the largest Kingdom of all. To pray and actually mean "thy Kingdom come," we must also be able to say "my kingdoms go." At best, most Christians split their loyalties between God and Caesar, but Francis and Clare did not. Their first citizenship was always, and in every case, elsewhere (Philippians 3:20), which ironically allowed them to live in this world with joy, detachment, and freedom.

THE GIFTS OF THE SIMPLE LIFE

We can summarize the transformative gifts of "leaving the world" in these ways:

When you agree to live simply, you put yourself outside of others' ability to buy you off, reward you falsely, or control you by money, status, salary, punishment, and loss or gain of anything. This is the most radical level of freedom, but, of course, it is not easy to come by. It might be called foundational restorative justice, or primal solidarity with the mass of humanity and the earth. Francis and Clare created a life in which they had little to lose, no desire for gain, no loans or debts to pay off, and no luxuries that they needed or wanted. Most of us can only envy them.

When you agree to live simply, you have little to protect and no desire for acquisition, even for acquisition of any "moral capital." If you imagine you are better, holier, higher, more important to God than others, it is a very short step to justified arrogance or violence toward those others. In fact, it is almost inevitable. And this is why so many say that the history of low-level religion and the history of violence are the same history. If you eliminate such manufactured and desired superiority, religion can finally become nonviolent in thought, word, and deed. Francis and Clare were masters at it, and so nonviolence came quite naturally to them and to the early movement they spawned.

When you agree to live simply you can understand what Francis meant when he said, "A brother has not given up all things if he holds onto the purse of his own opinions."[5] Most of us find out that this purse is far more dangerous and disguised than a money purse, and we seldom let go of it.

When you agree to live simply, you do not consider the immigrant, the refugee, the homeless person, or the foreigner as a threat to you or see them as being in competition with you. You have chosen their marginal state for yourself—freely and consciously becoming "visitors and pilgrims" in this world, as Francis puts it (quoting 1 Peter 2:11). A simple lifestyle is quite simply an act of solidarity with the way most people have lived since the beginnings of humanity. It is thus restorative justice instead of the world's limited notion of retributive justice.[6]

When you voluntarily agree to live simply, you do not need to get into the frenzy of work for the sake of salary or the ability to buy nonessentials or raise your social standing. You enjoy the freedom of *not climbing*. You might climb for others, but not just for yourself. (At least we can hope that is the case by the second half of life, which is what it should mean to be an elder.) The involuntarily poor, of course, must seek to climb at least a bit beyond survival all of their lives, and these are the ones who need our assistance and support.

When you agree to live simply, you have *time* for spiritual and corporal works of mercy because you have renegotiated in your mind and heart your very understanding of time and its purposes. Time is *not* money anymore, despite the common aphorism! Time is life itself.

When you agree to live simply, you can easily find a natural solidarity with all people on the edge and the bottom—the excluded, the shamed, and the forgotten—because you stop idealizing the climb and finally realize there isn't a top anyway.

When you agree to live simply, you have little energy to "circle the wagons" around your group, your ethnicity, your country, your money, and your religion. Your circle is no longer defined by these external and accidental qualities, because you are now finding the joy of the real Essentials and the actual Center—and, like all beauty, it is mostly *inside*.

When you agree to live simply, all the ideological "-isms" lose their pull and attraction: consumerism, classism, sexism, capitalism, ageism, lookism, communism, patriotism, fascism, even addiction, because they are all based on what John calls "disordered desire, lust of the eyes, and pride in possession...based on a world that is passing away" (1 John 2:16–17). As Pope Francis also says, reality is more important than our ideas about reality, which are mere "conceptual elaborations" which finally mask reality from itself.[7]

When you agree to live simply, the ethics and economics of war reveal themselves in all their evil and stupidity. Some say security systems, weapons, and armies actually demand 80 percent of the world's resources, and everything else is made to fall into place behind that. How could that possibly be the will of God? Wars are initiated by imperial thinking. Only people intent on their own protection and their own material advantage need wars and war economies (which is the only kind of economy we now have). A Christian can only tolerate clearly defensive attempts to protect the defenseless and the innocent. War must be the very last resort after all other means have truly been tried.

When you agree to live simply, people cease to be possessions and objects for your consumption or use. Your lust for relationships or for others to serve you, your need for other people's admiration, your desire to use other people as a kind of commodity for your personal pleasure, or any need to control and manipulate other people, slowly—yes, very slowly—falls away.

When you agree to live simply, there is no long-standing basis for any kind of addiction. You are free to enjoy, but you never let any enjoyment become your master. *You practice non-addiction every day by letting go, not needing, and not desiring anything in particular.* Fasting, detachment, and simplicity were the original words for non-addiction in the spiritual traditions.[8]

Yes, it is no exaggeration to say that Francis and Clare found a way out of the system, and a way that worked joyfully besides. But it also demanded that *they* first change in fundamental ways, rather than, as is so often the case now, that it is always *others* who need to change. Sometimes it is necessary to rail against injustice, however, and we should never undercut or fail to support such needed prophecy, especially when it is done in the nonviolent spirit of Jesus. But instances of true and full prophetic witness are somewhat rare, in my opinion. We often settle for just liberal or conservative politics.

The Soft Prophecy of Franciscanism

Franciscan prophecy is at its core "soft prophecy"—which is often the hardest of all! This is the prophecy of a way of life that is counter to the ways of the world; it is what I am calling "holy foolishness." I personally have found that few of us can offer "hard prophecy" from a truly clean heart and humble spirit. Any "against" kind of energy really makes you feel morally superior—and then gives you a false sense of standing for something important! We now call it "identity politics." It usually has more to do with our own self-image than with service or actual caring for others. Seeking to "clean the inside of our own dish," as Matthew puts it (23:26), before we try to clean other peoples' dishes is less politically correct, visible, or heroic. And, therefore, less common.

The teaching of soft prophecy became a primary reason why we founded the Center for Action and Contemplation in Albuquerque in 1987. The teaching and seeking of the contemplative mind, by solid contemplative practice, became the only effective way to integrate the inner with the outer journey. The result is summed up in one of our eight core principles: *"The best criticism of the bad is the practice of the better."*⁹ This approach guards against the most common criticism of religion in general and social-justice work in particular, which, frankly, has tended to produce many negative, oppositional, and judgmental people—from reactionary conservatives to limousine liberals. It has given Christianity a very bad name in much of the world, and seldom looks or feels like love.

Soft prophecy, which I first learned from Francis, moves all religion from any kind of elitism to the most egalitarian worldview of all, the broadest and biggest viewpoint possible, *the harmony of goodness itself—and where goodness is its own inherent reward*—which is always beautiful in people and yet also demands a basic change in attitude. For some reason, "doing charity" to get a reward later became much more common among Christians. This might get the job done, but it is not so beautiful and not very healing for those who receive our charity.

We lost our unique and prophetic way when we turned Brother Francis into "Saint Francis" and it was no longer considered foolish to say that you followed either Jesus or Francis and were living on the "edge of the inside"; in fact, it became fashionable, tame, sweet, and safe. A prophet's lifestyle is never fashionable or safe, but plaster saints usually are.

With that, we must move to the laboratory where all such radical change can occur—inside of our very mind, heart, and the cells of our body. I call it the laboratory of contemplative practice, which rewires our inner life and actually confirms in the soul a kind of "emotional sobriety"[10] plus an inner sense of divine union so we can do the needed works of justice with both peace and enduring passion.

CHAPTER FOUR

Home Base: Nature and the Road

Toward little worms even he glowed with a very great love...
he picked them up from the road and placed them in a safe
place, lest they be crushed by the feet of the passersby.[1]

—Thomas of Celano

He rejoiced in all the works of the hands of the Lord and saw
behind things pleasant to behold their life-giving reason
and cause. In beautiful things he saw Beauty itself; all things
were to him good.[2]

—Thomas of Celano

Let us place our first step at the bottom, presenting to ourselves
the whole material world as a mirror through which we may
pass over to God.[3]

—Bonaventure

Although I have been using the phrase "beyond the birdbath" as
a foil by which to distinguish authentic Franciscan spirituality from

its cheap counterfeits, there is also a reason that the images of Francis in the garden and with animals took over in art, memory, and poetry. Many seem to feel that Francis looks more at home in the yard than in the sanctuary—and it seems he often did, judging from the quotes that begin this chapter.

THE SACRAMENTAL MEANING OF THE WORLD

In stories of his life, Francis is quoted as talking to or about larks, lambs, rabbits, pheasants, falcons, cicadas, waterfowl, bees, the famous wolf of Gubbio, pigs whom he praised for generously giving their bodies for our food, and hooked fish that he tried to throw back into the water whenever possible. He addresses inanimate creation too, as if it were indeed ensouled, which we know because his "Canticle of the Creatures" includes fire, wind, water, Brother Sun, Sister Moon, and, of course, "our sister mother earth" herself. He even told the friars to only cut down part of a tree for their needs, so that it "might have hope of sprouting again."[4]

So-called "nature mysticism" was in fact a worthy first path for Francis, and also for Bonaventure who saw all things as *likenesses* of God (*vestigia Dei*), fingerprints and footprints that reveal the divine DNA underlying all living links in the Great Chain of Being. Both Francis and Bonaventure laid the foundation for what John Duns Scotus would later call "the univocity of all being," and what Dawn

Nothwehr, a Franciscan sister, calls "cosmic mutuality."[5]

Creation itself—not ritual or spaces constructed by human hands—was Francis's primary cathedral, which then drove him back into the needs of the city, very similar to Jesus's own movement between desert solitude and small-town healing ministry. The Gospel transforms us by putting us in touch with that which is much more constant and satisfying, literally the "ground of our being," and has much more "reality" to it, rather than theological concepts or the mere ritualization of reality. Daily cosmic events in the sky and on the earth are the Reality above our heads and beneath our feet every minute of our lives: a continuous sacrament. I find that a *preoccupation* with religious rituals tends to increase the more we remain untouched by Reality Itself—to which the best rituals can only point. Remember, even question 16 of the *Baltimore Catechism* answered firmly, clearly, and definitively that "God is everywhere!"

Jesus himself commonly points to things like the red sky, a hen, lilies, the fig tree, a donkey caught in a pit, the birds of the air, the grass in the field, the Temple animals which he released from their cages, and on and on. He was clearly looking at the seemingly "nonreligious" world, ordinary things all around him, and appeared to do most of his teaching outside. Francis said, "Wherever we are, wherever we go, we bring our cell with us. Our brother body is our cell and our soul is the hermit living in the cell. If our soul does not live in peace and solitude within this cell, of what avail is it to live in a man-made cell?"[6]

In the five-day Men's Rites of Passage[7] that was a focus of my work for fifteen years, so many men discovered that prayers and rituals inside of human-scale buildings made with artificial construction materials also came to seem very domesticated and controlled. They often perceived that the salvation offered there was also "small" and churchy. Almost without exception, the greatest breakthroughs for our men occurred during *extended times of silence in nature, where the human and the merely verbal were not in control—or during rituals that were raw and earthy.*

THE LOSS OF THE SACRAMENTALITY OF NATURE AFTER FRANCIS

Scholars say that the Franciscan movement following St. Francis himself was not really known for any deep connection with nature, except for some of the stories and sayings surrounding Anthony of Padua and Giles of Assisi. The first, short-lived generation dwelt in caves (*carceri*) and hermitages apart from the city, but we soon became gentrified and proper. I can remember my novice master in 1961 telling us we should not waste or consume or kill unnecessarily; but even such teachings were about private virtue and not presented as a social value or a necessity for the good of others. I never heard any direct teaching on sustainability or the sacramentality of nature itself in any of my thirteen formational years. We were trying to be Franciscans in the most developed, capitalized, and industrialized country in the world. "Sacraments" happened in church buildings, but not in the garden or the woods.

My thesis in this chapter is summed up by a quote from the Oxford scholar Roger Sorrell: "Possibly with the clericalization and sophistication of the Order, Francis's legacy lost its primary context and relevance. It was too easily intellectualized away by those removed (mentally and physically) from creation's sublimity to which Francis was so close, and with which he so intimately sympathized."[8] Once we lost regular contact with primal creation, I believe the Franciscan enterprise largely started to reflect whatever culture it inhabited, and that was no longer nature or the universe.

The chosen and preferred home base for many Franciscans when I first joined appeared to be books, offices, the academy, and almost always the sacristy. Our professors taught us Latin and Greek instead of any pastoral languages. I can only remember a couple of friars, of those who formed me, who had a garden or seemed to care about flowers, nature, animals, the universe, or anything that grew or changed. We seemed to prefer certain things to growing things, maybe because we were not around children. In most communities, dogs or cats were forbidden. There was a deep loneliness and sadness, and often eccentricity in many friars, as a result, and celibacy was thus a huge mistake for their hearts and their basic humanity. Thank God there were enough exceptions to let us know that being human, male, celibate, and Franciscan could indeed work!

The sacramental meaning of the world was largely lost until its more recent rediscovery by seers that we usually think of as "secular," "mere" nature mystics, poets and artists: people like Chief Seattle, John Muir, Rachel Carson, William Wordsworth, John James Audubon, Walt Whitman, Wendell Berry, Annie Dillard, Aldo Leopold, Teilhard de Chardin, Thomas Berry, Ansel Adams, Sallie McFague, Ilia Delio, Bill Plotkin, Mary Oliver, and Brian Swimme, to name some of the more outstanding. We Catholics ended up limiting "sacramentals" to things like religious medals, blessed candles, and holy water, instead of honoring the inherent holiness of the earth ores, beeswax, and H_2O that actually formed them. Please think about that!

We limited the official church sacraments to seven (six for women, subtracting the sacrament of Holy Orders) when "there should be seven hundred," as an old man once said to me in Tanzania. We ended up actually *desacralizing* God's world without realizing it. The people we called pagans and animists actually had a head start on us, because they at least saw the world as filled with spirits, whereas our world became empty, foreign, and without any natural balm for the soul. Wild was always bad, domesticated was always good. Yet C.S. Lewis said of God (in the character of the lion, Aslan), "He's wild, you know!" Domesticated, of course, means subservient to us. We liked our world more than God's world, it seems.

For much of Christian history we preached inside of a disenchanted, small, and lonely universe where there was no natural holiness or inherent goodness in anything non-human or non-Christian. I thought Jesus was "the Savior of the world" (John 4:42). We then tried to fill up the loneliness with books and ideas, since the world beneath us and above us had become boring, merely functional, and not subject to the predictability we wanted.

We humans prefer order and even have "a blessed rage for order" as Wallace Stevens said—and yet nature rarely complies! It is no accident that there are now so many eccentric and emotionally ill people in our world. *They deem themselves insignificant after trying to live meaningfully inside of a universe that was itself meaningless.* It does not work. *And we Christians insisted on perfect order even after the crucifixion of Jesus had warned us about and promised us an extreme disorder.* We grasped for meaning in merely mental ways when it was all around us in tangible and visible ways. We failed to kiss the ground on which we stood and preferred to fly off into the heavens.

"The first level of perception," according to Bonaventure, "is toward exterior material objects," and only when we see respectfully and lovingly at that level can we "ascend" to his second and third levels of full spiritual seeing.[9] Francis knew and taught that "God did not lose energy by plunging into form," as Cynthia Bourgeault so force-fully puts it,[10] and that true transcendence is to be found in immanence and materiality itself. What a surprise. But most of us were Platonists, where body and soul are enemies, much more than Christian incarna-tionalists, where body and soul were friends.[11] And where were we to experience this incarnation? Precisely *everywhere and all the time*, and not just in places defined as sacred, special, churchy, or religious. That is why Paul could confidently tell us we could and should "pray always."

ON THE ROAD, NOT IN THE MONASTERY

Nevertheless, despite the fading of the Franciscan emphasis on the sacramentality of nature, we have always been to a certain degree "non-churchy" when compared to many church groups—while still inte-grated within the social phenomenon of church, community, and ordi-nary neighborhood life. "Transcend and include" is the mature principle here: *we* let the church hold us in place and then move out from there! *Franciscans at their best attempted to live inside the universal mystery of "church" and from there we went out to serve the world.* Most Christians got it backward by living in the "world" and occasionally "going to church." I believe there is a creative tension between solid ground and the larger horizons we can see. Franciscan spirituality is "a sidewalk spirituality" for the streets of the world and the paths of the forest. It is not primarily based in the monastery, in church buildings, or in any asceticism or celibacy, despite all of our attempts to confine it there.

Scholars who have done a day-by-day study of Francis's earliest biographies have concluded that he lived *a very small part* of his year in actual community. This was shocking to those of us trained exclusively in what had become monastic community! This was the subject of my bachelor's thesis in 1965. Francis spent most of his time on the road and in the woods for "Lents," hermitages, island solitudes, and traveling between towns.[12] He seems to have traversed central and scenic Italy many, many times, visiting scores of towns. He also went to Syria, Egypt, and Spain with one or two others. It does not seem he had much time for "community" as we now think of it. Rather, his life illustrated the "two or three gathered in my name" that was Jesus's first definition of church.

After the initial golden age when the friars lived in wattles and woods, most of later Franciscan history rested on a strange three-legged tripod, as Franciscan Sister Ilia Delio puts it: The theology after the Council of Trent belonged to Thomas Aquinas (not Bonaventure or John Duns Scotus), the form of life belonged to St. Benedict (we called our friaries "monasteries" until my early years!), while the charism (that is, our animating spirit) was still *romantically* held by Francis. But we had neither the learned experience nor the living structures to communicate our unique charism with any distinctive vitality or message. Franciscan men became mostly priests of the church, women either teachers or nurses for church institutions, and these gave us our primary identity and security.[13] All fine, but not uniquely Franciscan or on the edge of the inside. We were fully inside.

PLUSES AND MINUSES

My early formation circled around monastic-choir obligations instead of any risky itineraries that took me out into nature or any "urban plunges" as we later called them. Most of my professors were academics, and I am deeply grateful for all they taught me, but now I am aware of what they did not teach me because they did not know it or enjoy it themselves. Few of them would have been at home among the poor or the outcasts, or camping out. I remember my disappointment when I was severely reprimanded by a friar professor for picking up a hitch-hiker as I drove the professor home from the airport. I had expected him to praise me! What was originally on the edge had been coopted to the conformist center. I encourage you to read the first Gospel descriptions of Jesus's sending of his disciples (Matthew 10:6–16, Luke 9:1–6, Mark 6:7–13), and to ask yourself how we Franciscans got from this vulnerable life on the road to the *ascribed status and security* we enjoy today—and which is so lethal for the male psyche and spirit.

One Franciscan professor of mine said that the Rule of St. Francis could basically be described as Tips for the Road in comparison to the beautiful Rule of St. Benedict, which is guidance and plan for a stable community. As G.K. Chesterton put it, "What Benedict stored, Francis scattered."[14] Francis's approach is much riskier, and has frankly led to a lot of Franciscan life that has had little discipline, clear direction, or proper boundaries.

We were seldom authoritarian, but that only works if you support it with true mentorship, eldering, and strongly internalized values. In my experience, the young ego is often left unformed and unchallenged, and there have been many human and spiritual casualties as a result. This gift of freedom makes formation into such a lifestyle rarer and much more difficult, and much more dependent on healthy models and elders *on site* (which is frankly rare). Monastic stability and structure has the real edge here. As I say in *Falling Upward*, you need to find a strong container in the first half of life, and Franciscan men, by our very love of freedom, often fail to provide that container. We are often so afraid of being authoritarian that we fail to be elders, guides, and real spiritual fathers to the young who want that very thing—usually without knowing it. And then they leave disillusioned.

So our Franciscan strength may also be our weakness. Ignatius of Loyola (1491–1556) later tried to bring inner discipline and self-initiative to religious life, with many good results. If a Franciscan does not strongly internalize his or her vocation, our way of life is highly open to whimsy, floating, and unfettered egocentricity in the name of gospel freedom. Francis called such friars "drones" and vagabonds, and encouraged them to change or leave. Did you ever notice that it is usually friars' smiling faces that are put on wine and beer bottles, and their rotund, brown-robed figures are often made into happy, potbellied cookie jars and cartoon characters? What a telling public image we seem to enjoy!

Franciscanism has always been ethos or spirit, more than rule or schedule, which is good, but also dangerous for those who are lazy, unconverted, or unmotivated. If you do not really meet and fall in love with Jesus, you can largely live for yourself and still think of this as a "religious life." Even the vow of poverty can create a well-disguised welfare state that encourages codependency and discourages personal responsibility and initiative. Gospel freedom is always a risk, and only the mature can handle it well.

Chapter three of Francis's Rule of 1223 totally assumes an itinerant worldview, "going about the world," and never riding horseback (a mode of travel that was for the rich in his time). He advised the friars that "whatever house you enter say 'Peace to this house,'" and "eat whatever is set before you." There were no dietary rules either, just as in the

Gospels, but only enjoying "whatever table the Lord provides"—except that Francis himself ate far too little. It was only at the very end of his life that he "spoke joyfully to his body," and asked "Brother Body" for forgiveness with the firm promise that he "would now give heed to his complaints."[15]

Begging (mendicancy), which was central to the first Franciscans, implied being among the people and identified with the bottom and not the top, living in the cities, and working with laborers in farms and towns: *in a role of neediness rather than being needed ourselves.* That sense of need deeply affects the soul when you are the receiver instead of always being the giver. University settings, huge churches, and larger "monastery" buildings came much later, but would have been abhorrent to the first generation, as we see in Francis's violent reaction to the tiled friaries the brothers tried to build in Bologna and at the Portiuncula. "Friars" were to be different than "monks" and friaries inspired a different lifestyle than monasteries, not based on schedule and order but on personal contact with ordinary people, ongoing conversion, and concrete works of service for those who could not pay us back. But of course that does not pay the bills or sustain institutions. Such vulnerability is much harder to teach, model, or perpetuate. It has always left us in a very fragile position in terms of passing on our charism, as I think we are experiencing now—just when the world needs us so much.

Rediscovering the Heart of Franciscanism

But it is still *ours* to rediscover and reenergize our own Franciscan charism, as Vatican II exactly and directly told us to do.[16] The religious sisters of all orders seem to be doing it the best, and this is probably why they have recently been such a threat to those who define faith as certitude, nostalgia, or the maintaining of social order. The true Gospel always leaves us both fragile and vulnerable, or as Jesus said, "as sheep among wolves" (Matthew 10:16). Yet this is exactly what the world wants and expects from Franciscans, and for what Jesus freed us, so we cannot lose heart. I find that people today are quite ready to hear messages of simplicity, nonviolence, humility, structural insecurity, love of animals and "enemies," and even expect basic earth care from us. In fact, they are deeply disappointed when we are merely priests in brown robes who reflect current cultural values, upward mobility, and church more than Gospel.

I was once told that two Christian groups carry the least negative baggage in Western civilization: Franciscans and Quakers! When Patrick Carolan, who is executive director of the Franciscan Action Network, spoke at the United Nations in June 2013, the avowed communist who chaired the international meeting said warmly and publicly in conclusion, "And may God bless you for your good work."

Murmuring and surprise filled the General Assembly because the word *God* is seldom used in formal sessions at the UN. In fact, it is almost *verboten*. Yet a secular Franciscan spokesman who was humbly talking on climate change and jobs for the poor called forth this amazing response from a formal unbeliever. That is Franciscan evangelization: not preaching at or to people, but just making the truth beautiful, attractive, and warm.

If Franciscans go back to our contemplative, simple living and peace-making foundations, we might again look like the Catholic version of the Quakers and the Amish, who often look like we initially looked, it seems to me. The world expects and longs for a truly unique, positive, and inviting message from the children of St. Francis. I have found this to be true—without exception—on all continents where I have taught and preached. They are disappointed when we are just like everybody else and a lazy conformity has again won out over the revolutionary character of the Gospel.

When I am introduced as a priest, as an American, as a man, as educated, there are the usual blank, unexpectant faces, and often bored resignation; but the moment the speaker says, "He is a Franciscan," faces turn toward me and light up with some kind of hope, and often even smile. This is really true! We must not be robbed of such a "straight path and open highway" (Matthew 3:3). It invites us and allows us to do much good in our world—far beyond our actual numbers or importance.

CHAPTER FIVE
. . . .

Contemplation: A Different Way of Knowing

We must know spiritual things spiritually.

—1 Corinthians 2:13

IN CHAPTER THREE, WE SAW how Francis and Clare chose to live on the "edge of the inside," a very different place from the lives of most of us who want to be front and center. But why, even from that position, do you think that they were able to see things so differently? Was it because they were more moral, more "chosen," more detached, more loving, more sincere? These are all likely true, yet I believe the very foundation of what we mean by holiness, or, in this case, mysticism, is that they knew and loved from a different source; they knew by *participation in a Larger Knowing that many of us call God*. Or, as Paul says, "They knew as fully as they were known" (1 Corinthians 13:12).

This kind of shared knowing, which is nothing but full consciousness (conscire = consciousness*) is what many of us mean by contemplation.* True contemplatives surrender some of their own ego boundaries and identity so that God can see through them, with them, and in them—with a larger pair of eyes. It is quite simply a higher level of seeing, and, if you do not like the religious language, you can just call it consciousness, or deep consciousness. But you still have to let go of your small, egoic self to get there (John 12:24).

You have surely wondered why some people understand spiritual things in a much more compelling way than the rest of us do. They believe the same doctrines that we do, but their faith is alive and changes both their minds and their hearts in obvious ways. Many of us think we get the "what" of a doctrine, but it does not radically change us or inspire others. As Jesus says, "it is merely a lesson memorized" (Matthew 15:9). Big Truth is intended to deeply change the seer himself or herself, or it is not Big Truth—or truth at all. Some form of contemplative practice is the key to this larger seeing and this larger knowing.

WHO IS DOING THE SEEING?

It comes down to this: When we see things in a unitive way, in conscious union with the eyes of God, what we see is qualitatively different. Basically, it is no longer self-referential but very expansive seeing, and this changes everything. This is what the true contemplative is seeking, and thus seeing, day after day.

Many see a supposedly good "new thing" but still in an old way, which is to say, with their old self, from the egoic position of self-advantage and self-importance. So the new thing is never really new; it is still "all about me." If the supposedly new thing has not been able to change my old self, others will rightly ask why it would change the world or why they should believe it is true. Why should anybody believe you? Yet so many did believe the new self and the new way that Francis and Clare exhibited. The self they became was humanly believable and beautiful, and that also made their moral choices trustworthy and true.

The result of contemplative sight is what I would like to call "beautiful" morality, and the lack of it is why so many of us dislike and mistrust so many supposedly "moral" people. Let me try to explain. To do a highly moral thing, such as caring for the earth, but with the wrong energy (in an angry, pushy, or know-it-all way), is a kind of ugly morality and not the "aroma" and "incense" of Christ (2 Corinthians 2:14–15). It is formally right, but somehow terribly wrong, and we sense it. Perhaps that is why so many religious and formally moral people do not seem attractive or happy to us.

To do a moral or virtuous thing, however, with the right energy is what I would call beautiful morality. Yet it will often be judged by the same kind of people who accused Jesus. This is precisely the vulnerability of the faith position, and why it takes the darkness of faith to be faithful. In other words, you must be open to the possibility that you are wrong.

Quite simply, the right energy comes forth when it is not "all about you," or about you being right, but radiates a further message, a larger presence, an inner vitality that shines through those very words and actions—and this becomes the core message itself! Most mature people can tell the difference immediately, without perhaps realizing why one action attracts and changes us, and the other repels us, even though both might be formally correct.[1]

Francis and Clare exemplify a truly beautiful morality, so much so in fact that it hardly feels like morality at all, but just a full and fresh humanity! Francis told us that we needed "to give people reasons for spiritual joy"[2] and not just quote commandments to them. Humans respond to one another's "infallible energies,"[3] as Mary Oliver calls them, much more than to their precise words or actions. True morality always feels very unselfconscious. It is precisely *not* "all about me" but about the issue itself or about others.

Beautiful morality even shines forth when someone does an imperfect thing (as almost all actions are), but the energy of the person is filled with love for others, a kind of self-effacement and humility about the outcome of the issue itself, and his or her own opinion about it. I have met very fundamentalist Christians who hold some very rigid moral conclusions, but they hold their position on things like drinking, war, or gay people with such humility, soft-spokenness, and kindness that you know they have the *spirit* of Jesus nonetheless—while others might have very good "theology," but their life energy is all too glib, smug, and self-satisfied. It is right, but somehow still wrong. It does not have the aroma of Christ.

The motivation, meaning, and inherent energy of any action comes from its ultimate source, which is the person's *foundational and core vantage point*. What is his or her real and honest motivation? "Who" is doing the seeing? Is it the "cut-off branch," the egoic self, trying to do the seeing (John 15:5)? Is it a person needing to be right or is it a person who wants to love? There is a very different kind of seeing from a branch that has remained lovingly and consciously connected to its Source (God, Jesus, our Higher Power). When Jesus spoke of a "cut-off branch," he meant a person who can only see from its small position of "me" and what meets "my" needs. It seems to me our society is largely populated by such cut-off branches, where a commitment to the common and real good has become almost a rarity.

Seeing from a pair of glasses beyond our own is what I call "*participative seeing.*" This is the new self that can say excitedly with Paul, "I live no longer, not 'I' but it is Christ now living in me" (Galatians 2:20). In the truest sense, *I am that which I am seeking.* This primal communion

immediately *communicates* a spaciousness, a joy, and a quiet content-
ment. It is not anxious, because the essential gap between me and the
world has already been overcome. I am at home, and I do not need to
prove myself to anybody, nor do I need to be "right," nor do you have
to agree with me.

A mature believer, of course, knows that it is impossible *not* to be
connected to the Source, or to be "on the Vine," as Jesus says. But most
people are not consciously there yet. They are not "saved" from themselves, which is the only thing we really need to be saved from. They do
not yet live out of their objective, totally given, and unearned identity,
"hidden with Christ in God" (Colossians 3:3). This is what saints like
Francis and Clare allowed, enjoyed, and "fell into." It is always a falling!
For most of us, our own deepest identity is still well hidden from us.[4]
*Religion's primary and irreplaceable job is to bring this foundational truth
of our shared identity in God to full and grateful consciousness.* This is the
only true meaning of holiness.

The vast majority of humanity and a large percentage of Christians
and clergy have not grasped this wondrous truth, and there are even
fewer who dare to enjoy it even after they have heard it might be true.
As we say, it "goes right over their heads" and beyond their hearts. The
irony is that this "holiness" is actually our "first nature," yet we made it
so impossible that it did not even become our "second nature" that we

could easily wear with dignity. This core Christ identity was made into a worthiness contest, or a moral contest, at which almost no one wins and so most do not even try. Francis and Clare undid the whole contest by rejoicing in their ordinariness and seeming unworthiness—which I believe is the core freedom of the Gospel itself. And I must say it again: this is something you can only fall into and receive—and nothing that you can achieve, which utterly humiliates the ego, the willful, and all overachievers.

PAUL'S SERMON ON WISDOM

To help you work toward these central issues of identity, contemplation, and participation, and to further explain what I mean by mysticism itself, I look to a central teaching from Paul, which some have rightly called his *sermo sapientiae*, or "sermon on wisdom" (1 Corinthians 1:17–3:3). I am not aware that early Franciscans quoted these passages directly that much, but they surely lived the message. Here, Paul first recognizes that many of his new converts were doing spiritual things, but still in very immature and *unspiritual* ways (for example, to feel or look holy, to cultivate a positive self-image, to "get" God's love, or to "earn" entry into heaven). He calls them "infants in Christ" who are not yet ready for "solid food" (1 Corinthians 3:2). (I am assuming that anyone who would bother with this book is someone ready for solid food, and that is you!) Many of us today seem to recognize that we have settled for religion as attendance at something, or belonging to some-thing, which would surely be baby food, instead of religion as *inherently participating in something*.

"Understanding spiritual things spiritually" is Paul's summary statement about a different form of nutrition that he calls "spiritual knowing" or "wisdom" and which he opposes to "folly." As he so often does, Paul uses a paradoxical contrast to teach his major points. He will do the same in other places with other seeming opposites (flesh or Spirit, Adam or Christ, death or life, Jew or Greek, and law or grace), in each case to bring us to a new synthesis on a higher level. Francis and Clare did the same thing with poverty and riches, suffering and joy, and self-abandonment and freedom. Paul's paradox of wisdom and foolishness teaches us how to begin to think non-dually or "mystically" ourselves, and mature Christians pick up his brilliant style of thinking.

Consciously, trustfully, and lovingly remaining on "the Vine" (John 15:1) which is to be connected to our Source, is precisely our access point to deeper spiritual wisdom. We know by participation with and in God, which creates our very real co-identity with Christ: *We are also both human and divine, as he came to reveal and model.* The foundational meaning of transformation is to surrender to this new identity and to consciously draw upon it.

In short, we must change our *very self-image rather than just be told some new things to see or do*. To be a Christian is to objectively know that we share the same identity that Jesus enjoyed as both human and divine, which is what it means to "follow" him. I, in fact, believe that *this is the whole point of the Gospel and the Incarnation!* (Read John 14 and 15 in their entirety, lest you think I am overstating my position, or study the early Fathers of the Eastern Church, who got this much more clearly than the Western Church.)

This realization that Someone is living in us and through us is exactly how we plug into a much larger mind and heart beyond our own. Afterward, we know in a different way, although we have to keep relearning this truth over and over again (which is probably the point of daily prayer). But it demands a major dying of our small self, our ego, and maybe that is why so few go there. As Jesus clearly puts it, one "self" must die for another "Self" to be born; that message is quite explicit in all four Gospels (Mark 8:35; Luke 9:24; Matthew 16:25; John 12:24). In the practical order, this mostly feels like taking my "self," my ego— both its hurts and its importance, which are largely manufactured by my mind—less seriously day by day. Growth in salvation is growth in liberation from the self.

I want to say very clearly that this "foundational holiness" or ontological union with God is our *first nature*, and is enjoyed by people who are still psychologically or intellectually immature on other levels.[5] In fact, God has always—and only—been in union with an obviously imperfect humanity. That is the essential character of divine mercy. Salvation is always pure and total gift from God's side. Living and thinking autonomously, separately, or cut off from such a Vine or Source is what Paul means by being foolish and unspiritual, and living in union is precisely wisdom (more than just being "moral" about a rule or orthodox about a doctrine).

Separateness is unfortunately the chosen stance of the small self, which then has a hard time thinking paradoxically or living in unity—but always takes one side or the other in order to feel secure. It frames everything in a binary way: for me or against me, totally right or totally wrong, my group's opinion or another group's—all dualistic formulations. That is the best that the small egotistical self can do, and it is not anywhere close to adequate for God's full purposes. It might be an early level of intelligence, but it is never wisdom or spiritual intelligence.[6] The small self is still objectively in union with God, it just does not know it, or enjoy it, or draw upon it. "Is it not written in your own law, 'You are gods'?" (John 10:34). Don't accuse me of heresy here; Jesus said that! But for most of us, this objective divine *image* has not yet become the subjective *likeness*, to use the two helpful Genesis metaphors (1:26–27). Our goal is to illustrate both the *image* and the *likeness* of God. What a momentous vocation we humans have!

One must fully recognize that mystics like Francis and Clare were speaking from this place of conscious, chosen, and loving union with God, and such union was realized by *surrendering* to it and not by any *achieving* of it! Surrender to Another, participation with Another, and divine union are finally the same thing. Once we have achieved this union, we look out at reality from a much fuller Reality *that now has eyes beyond and larger than our own.* This is precisely what it means to "live in Christ" (*en Cristo*), to pray "through" Christ, or to do anything "in the name of God," phrases with which we are all quite familiar.

Such a letting go of our own small vantage point is the core of what we mean by conversion, but also what we mean by Franciscan "poverty." Poverty is not just a life of simplicity, humility, restraint, or even lack. Poverty is when we recognize that *myself—by itself—is powerless and ineffective.* John's Gospel puts it quite strongly when it says that a branch that does not abide in Jesus "is withered and useless" (John 15:6). The transformed self, living in union, no longer lives in shame or denial of its weakness, but even lives with rejoicing because it does not need to pretend that it is any more than it actually is—which is now more than enough! "When I am weak, I am strong," Paul says (2 Corinthians 12:10), to make the same point dramatically.

"OH! BLESSED RAGE FOR ORDER!"

In the practical order, contemplation gives us an inner capacity to live with paradoxes and contradictions. It is a quantum leap forward in our tolerance for ambiguity, mystery, and paradox. More than anything else, this new way of processing the moment is what moves us from mere intelligence, or correct information, to what we normally mean by wisdom or non-dual thinking.

Paul begins his sermon on wisdom in 1 Corinthians 1:17 by making a distinction between what both philosophers and Jews would call wisdom, and he tells us that neither of their definitions of wisdom can deal with disorder, absurdity, and the tragic, and thus fail to meet the test of true wisdom. He says only "the folly of the cross" can deal with what poet Wallace Stevens called "our blessed rage for order!" *The "mystery of the cross" is Paul's code-breaking and fundamental resolution for the confusing mystery of life!* Without it, it seems most people become cynics, depressed, bitter, or negative by the middle of life, because there is no meaning in the death of all things and the imperfection of everything. For Paul, the deepest level of *meaning* is ironically the deep, grace-activated acceptance of a certain *meaninglessness*! We are able to leave room for God to fill in the gaps, and even trust that God will! This new leap of logic is often called faith. I believe such contemplative seeing, or wisdom, actually sharpens your capacity for true reason and logic, because your ego is now out of the way. Don't deny that until you have tried it yourself. Faith does not allow for theoretical rejection.

Paul knows that some will insist on law to maintain their view of order ("Jews" or "conservatives"), while others will try to use intellect to create some kind of order and meaning to their universe ("Greeks" or "liberals"). But he insists that neither of them can finally succeed, because they do not have the ability to "incorporate the negative," which is always there. *The greatest enemy of ordinary daily goodness and joy is not imperfection, but the demand for some supposed perfection.* Please meditate on that. There seems to be a dark side to almost everything, but only the unitive or non-dual mind can accept this and not panic, but, in fact, grow because of it.

These two classic patterns of liberal and conservative are perennial, taking different names in each age and culture (romantic versus rational or Plato versus Aristotle, for example). Each stance is *good and necessary as far as it can go. But neither of them can deal with disorder and misery in any form.* Paul believes that Jesus has revealed the only response that works. The revelation of the cross, he says, makes you indestructible, because it says that there is a way through all absurdity and tragedy, and that way is precisely through accepting absurdity and tragedy as part of God's unfathomable agenda. If you internalize the mystery of the cross, you will not fall into cynicism, failure, bitterness, or skepticism. I have met such souls all over the world. The cross gives you a precise and profound way through the dark side of life and through all disappointments. Without it, most harden and retreat.

The revelation of the cross is exactly how Jesus "breaks the bonds of death" as our Easter songs love to say. *Your wounds can no longer wound you once you gaze upon the crucified and let him return his message from the cross.* I believe there are three central messages that Jesus speaks directly from the cross:

1. That you will and must face a feeling of "forsakenness" (Mark 15:34).
2. That you must eventually be able to say "Father, forgive them, they know not what they do" (Luke 23:34).
3. That you must end your life by saying, "Into your hands, O Lord, I entrust my spirit" (Luke 23:46). For many that comes only in the last moments.

These are the essential last words preceding all resurrection. Jesus could not promise us resurrection (John 11:25–26) without also telling us how to get there. And the pathway is toward full and eternal liberation.

THE PARADOXICAL REVELATION OF THE CROSS
So Paul allows both conservatives and liberals to define wisdom in their own ways, yet dares to call both of them inadequate and finally wrong because such worldviews will eventually fail them: "God has shown up human wisdom as folly" on the cross (1 Corinthians 1:21), and this is "an obstacle that the Jews [his own people] cannot get over," and which

the gentiles or pagans think is simple "foolishness" (1:23). These world-views, for Paul, indeed end up being foolish themselves because even perfect laws, courtrooms, and brilliant intellect cannot and will not be able to deal with the broken, imperfect world, the tragic "fly in the oint-ment" of reality. Look how institutions like the Supreme Court, our legislative bodies, and our universities promise order and truth, and still create such cynical people. They can never bring about the utopia that we all desire. They can achieve some degree of retributive justice, but only God's healing love, coming through people, can achieve restor-ative justice.

Each worldview has its own folly and its own form of wisdom, and Paul says the cross has challenged both and comes out with the best and most honest answer—precisely *because it incorporates the tragic (the irrational, absurd, and sinful) and uses it for good purposes.* In his thinking, only the Christian perspective can absorb and appreciate paradox—which is order within disorder, redemption through tragedy, resurrec-tion through death, divinity through humanity. For him, therefore, *the cross and its transformative power* is his summary symbol for the depths of divine wisdom, which seems like mere "folly" to the "masters of every age" (1 Corinthians 2:6). The compassionate holding of essential mean-inglessness or tragedy, as Jesus does in hanging on the cross, is the final and triumphant resolution of all the dualisms and dichotomies that we ourselves must face in our own lives. We are thus "saved by the cross"!

Paradox held and overcome is the beginning of training in non-dual thinking or contemplation, as opposed to paradox denied, which forces us to choose only one part of any mysterious truth. Such a choice will be false because we usually choose the one that serves our small purposes. Who would ever choose the cross? Yet life often demands it of us anyway.[7] Would anyone ever willingly choose to have a Down Syndrome child? Yet how many of such families rise to very high levels of love and compassion, including the other children in the family? Paul offers a wisdom not to Jews *or* pagans, but to both Jews *and* pagans, whom he calls to see things through wisdom eyes.

Conversion, therefore, is not joining a different group, but seeing with the eyes of the crucified. The cross is Paul's philosopher's stone or "code breaker" for any lasting spiritual liberation. God can save sincere people of faith inside of any system or religion, if only they can be patient, trusting, and compassionate in the presence of human misery or failure, especially their own. This is life's essential journey. These trustful ones have surrendered to Christ, very often without needing to use the precise word "Christ" at all (Matthew 7:21). It is the doing not the saying that matters.

THE LOSERS WIN

Paul's exciting and bold proclamation is then that "God's folly is wiser than human wisdom, and God's weakness is stronger than human strength" (1 Corinthians 1:25). He says that only Spirit can hold and absorb the seeming contradictions and allow us to see and to *know* from an utterly new and *unitive* vantage point, which is the deepening fruit of contemplation. Only Spirit-in-us can know non-dually or paradoxically and absorb contradictions inside of and with God. Only God's Spirit-with-us can fully forgive, accept, and allow reality to be what it is. Neither logic nor law can fully achieve this, but *participation with and in* God can. (This does not make logic or law unnecessary; they are simply inadequate to the work of transformation).

In the practical order this means that *we all must learn to offer life a foundational yes before we offer our critical no. If we start with no, it is almost impossible to ever get back to a full yes.*

This is humiliating to all thinking people, except to those who have "walked through the valley of the shadow of death" (Psalm 23:4) themselves and "know" in a new way, almost unbeknownst to themselves! You have all met such people, but they are usually quiet, often "uneducated," and even "unimportant." I meet a lot of them in the recovery programs, at the senior center, and in the county jail, to be honest. Just recently, I talked to a recovering drug addict who had survived an early life of abuse that led him to his addiction. Yet he had nothing but respect for goodness itself, which he now seemed to see everywhere— plus a deep humility and honesty about himself. Any little bit of love or

"God language" went a long way with this middle-aged man, just the opposite of our terribly entitled society—and even church society. But what a price he had to pay for such wisdom and such freedom.

THE TRANSFORMED ONES

Paul notes how a human person can only know him- or herself from the inside out, and a total outsider or mere observer cannot really know another. Then he rushes to his grand finale by saying that "nobody knows the qualities of God except the Spirit of God" (1 Corinthians 2:11). God knowledge must be an inside job! One does not ever look at God, *one only looks out from God*. One does not pray "to" Christ as much as one prays "Through Christ, our Lord, Amen!"

And then you can almost hear him shouting: "And YOU have God's own Spirit—by which you can understand the lavish gifts God has given us!" (1 Corinthians 2:12). *You and God are no longer two, but one! God in you knows. God in you loves.* This is "knowing spiritual things spiritually" and in this frame "no one can boast" (1 Corinthians 1:29) or take credit. It is always pure gift. Or, as John says, "He is with you, he is in you…he will teach you all things and *re-mind* you of all things!" (John 14:17, 26).

The contemplative mind, the wisdom way, the non-dual mystic thus has no need to either play the victim or create victims. This is the way God seems to turn the world on its head and allow simple good will to reign and win (not law, intelligence, or superiority of any kind, which appeal far too much to the ego's small purposes). The playing field of life, history, and culture has been absolutely leveled and liberated by the Gospel. All have, and always have had from the beginning, equal access to God; in fact, it is the little ones who have a great big head start: "So it was to shame the wise that God chose what is foolish by human reckoning, and to shame what is strong that he chose what is weak by human reckoning" (1 Corinthians 1:27).

This is not to defeat or lessen human effort or intelligence, for its effect is exactly the opposite; the goal of the Gospel is to elevate us to full participation in the divine, leading Paul in a few verses to say, "You are indeed God's farm, you are God's building.... God's temple is holy, and you are that temple!" (1 Corinthians 3:9, 17). Such inherent dignity only sharpens and grounds our use of our God-given mind.

Actual divine participation is all you need to know to be a contemplative, but you will need to draw upon this totally available gift (2 Peter 1:3–4) anew every day and in every way—and with a renewed eagerness that is itself a gift to be asked for. It is such a stupendous message that even much of the Christian tradition has chosen to ignore it, deny it, or make it into a moral contest where most refuse to even try because it seems so stacked in favor of a certain kind of temperament or personality ("churchy people"), who are often not that inspiring or believable to those outside.

Let me end by quoting Bonaventure who is quoting Augustine, who speaks directly to the human capacity for a true experiential union with God. I believe the joy that is at the heart of the Franciscan alleluia proceeds from this inner realization, which descends upon us at ever deeper levels as we walk our faith journey. This deepening is the only real goal of Christian contemplation, and is the heart of the Perennial Tradition of wisdom. This is how Francis and Clare, and all contemplatives, "know" things: *"The soul itself is an image of God, to which God is so present that the soul can actually grasp God, and 'is capable of possessing God and of being a partaker in God."*[8]

With that we can move forward. In fact, we can move far and wide and confidently forward.

CHAPTER SIX

An Alternative Orthodoxy:
Paying Attention to Different Things

Til the end of his life, Francis stated his right to interpret
his own charism himself, as illustrated by the fact that
he presented his own Testament as the sole authorized
commentary on his Rule.... When all is said and done, we
can say that the Church welcomed Francis and his brothers
without really understanding the whole import and meaning
of his message.[1]

—ANDRÉ VAUCHEZ

ONE OF THE EARLIEST ACCOUNTS of Francis, the "Legend of Perugia,"
quotes Francis as telling the first friars, "You only know as much as you
do."[2] His emphasis on action, practice and lifestyle was foundational
and revolutionary for its time and at the heart of Franciscan alternative orthodoxy ("heterodoxy"). For Francis and Clare, Jesus became
someone to actually imitate and not just to worship.

Up to this point, most of Christian spirituality was based in desert asceticism, monastic discipline, theories of prayer, or academic theology, which itself was often based in "correct belief" or liturgy, but not in a kind of practical Christianity that could be lived in the streets of the world. Many rightly say *Francis emphasized an imitation and love of the humanity of Jesus, and not just the worshiping of his divinity.* That is a major shift.

Those who have analyzed the writings of Francis have noted that he uses the word *doing* rather than *understanding* at a ratio of 175 times to five. *Heart* is used 42 times to one use of *mind*. *Love* is used 23 times as opposed to 12 uses of *truth*. *Mercy* is used 26 times while *intellect* is used only one time. This is a very new perspective that is clearly different from (and an antidote to) the verbally argumentative Christianity of his time, and from the highly academic theology that would hold sway for the next thousand years. He took prayer on the road and into the activity of life itself, as we saw in chapter four, which is why the Franciscans popularized the portable, small psalter that we still call the breviary.

A MINORITY POSITION

Throughout history, the Franciscan School has typically been a minority position inside of the Roman Catholic and larger Christian tradition, yet it has never been condemned or considered heretical—in fact, quite the opposite. It just emphasized different teachings of Jesus, new perspectives and behaviors, and focused on the full and final implications of the Incarnation of God in Christ. For Franciscans, the incarnation was not just about Jesus but was manifested everywhere once you learned how to see spiritually. As Francis said, "The whole world is our cloister"!

Early Franciscanism was sort of a para-church *on the edge of the inside* of organized Christianity, similar to others who had occupied that same location: desert fathers and mothers, many early monastics before they became clericalized and domesticated, Celtic Christianity, and even some religious orders down to our own time. Most Catholics are accustomed to such groups living on the side and the edge of the normal parish church system, but this is also why Francis has often been called "the first Protestant." He did what he did, however, from the inside and with no oppositional energy. How did he achieve this rare synthesis?

As we have seen in earlier chapters, Francis's starting place was human suffering instead of human sinfulness, and God's identification with that suffering in Jesus. That did not put him in conflict with any Catholic dogmas or structures. His Christ was cosmic while also deeply personal, his cathedral was creation itself, he preferred the bottom of society to the top. He invariably emphasized inclusion of the seeming outsider over any club of insiders, and he was much more a mystic than a moralist. In general, Francis preferred ego poverty to private perfection, because Jesus "became poor for our sake, so that we might become rich out of his poverty" (2 Corinthians 8:9). All of this was hard to question or criticize (although some still did, and still *do*, as we presently see in the critics of Pope Francis).

Francis's was a radically Christo-centric worldview, but one that nevertheless recognized the Church as the primary arena in which this good news could be protected and disseminated. He was a non-dual thinker. Francis did not need to prove to anyone that his church was the only or exclusive "Body of Christ." That problem had not yet developed, except between East and West. He instead saw the living Body of Christ, first of all, *everywhere*, and then the organized Church was where that "hidden Mystery" could most easily be recognized, talked about, developed, and praised. Most of us come at it from the other side, "My church is better than your church," and never get to the real universal message. We substitute the container for the actual contents, and often substitute our church structure for the Gospel or the kingdom of God. Francis was an extraordinary "yes, and" kind of man, which kept him from all negativity toward structures or other groups.

For Francis, if Jesus himself was humble and poor, then the pure and simple imitation of Jesus became his life's agenda. In fact, he often did it in an almost slavishly literal way. He was a fundamentalist, not about doctrinal Scriptures, but about *lifestyle Scriptures* ("Take nothing for your journey," "Eat what is set before you," "Work for your wages," "Wear no shoes."). This is still revolutionary thinking for most Christians, although it is the very "marrow of the Gospel," to use Francis's own phrase, because he knew what many educators have now proven—that *humans tend to live themselves into new ways of thinking more than think themselves into new ways of living.* The lecture method changes very few people at any deep or long-lasting level. It normally does not touch the unconscious, where all our hurts and motives lie hidden and disguised.

"When we are weak, we are strong" (2 Corinthians 12:10) might have been the motto of the early Franciscans. In chapter nine of his First Rule, Francis wrote, "They should be glad to live among social outcasts."[3] Biblically, they reflected the primitive and practical Christianity found in the Letter of James and the heart-based mysticism of the Eastern Church. Most male Franciscans eventually became clericalized and proper churchmen, but we did not begin that way.[4]

The more radical forms of Christianity have never thrived for very long, starting with Pentecost itself and the first "sharing of all things in common" (Acts 2:44–45), the desert fathers and mothers, and the early Celtic monastics; continuing through groups like the Waldensians, the Beguines and Beghards, the Bruderhof, the Amish, and many others; down to the Catholic Workers and the Sant'Egidio Community in our own time. Unless such groups become strongly institutionalized, and even juridical about it, they tend to be short-lived or very small, but always wonderful experiments that challenge the rest of us. They are always like *a new room with a new view* offering the rest of us an essential viewpoint that we have lost.

How Can Orthodoxy Be Alternative?

Perhaps these descriptions of Franciscan alternative orthodoxy strike you as unusual, impossible, or even oxymoronic. "Either they are orthodox (right and true) or they are not," you might say. How can Franciscanism be an alternative and still be called orthodox? *But "heterodoxy" is precisely a third something in between orthodoxy and heresy!* I sincerely think Francis found a creative Third Way, which is the creative and courageous role of a prophet and a mystic. *He basically repeated what all prophets say, that the message and the medium for the message have to be the same thing.* And Francis emphasized the medium itself, instead of continuing to clarify or contain the mere verbal message (which tends to be the "priestly" job). As a result, Francis, like all true prophets, has much more historical and social impact than priests usually do, who in their preoccupation with protecting and maintaining the status quo often miss out on both the true Tradition and its unfolding in history.[5]

The early Franciscan friars and "Poor Clares" wanted to be *Gospel practitioners* instead of merely "word police," "inspectors," or "museum curators" as Pope Francis calls some clergy. Both Francis and Clare offered their rules as a *forma vitae*, or "form of life," to use their own words. They saw orthopraxy ("correct practice") as a necessary parallel, and maybe even precedent, to mere verbal orthodoxy ("correct teaching") and not an optional add-on or a possible implication. History has shown that a rather large percentage of Christians never get to the practical implications of their beliefs! "Why aren't you doing what you say you believe?" the prophet invariably asks.

Every viewpoint is a view from a point. One group's terrorist is another group's freedom fighter. One group's devout friar is another group's dangerous heretic. But the Franciscan School found a positive and faith-filled way around such dualistic and self-serving thinking. They found a way to be both very traditional and very revolutionary at the same time by emphasizing practice over theory. At the heart of their orthopraxy was the practice of *paying attention to different things* (nature, the poor, humility, itinerancy, the outsider, mendicancy, mission instead of shoring up the home base, and the Gospels "without gloss," as Francis put it). In doing so, without fighting about creedal statements, they created a very different *imaginarium* (the unconscious container inside of which each group does its thinking) for many people. For more on this, see chapter sixteen.

They also *de-emphasized* other things (big churches, priesthood, liturgy as theater instead of prayer, ostentation of any kind, seeking church offices, hierarchical titles and costumes), perhaps because they saw other groups emphasizing these very things. Today, as throughout history, the Franciscan *imaginarium* is very different from that of most bishops and diocesan priests. How could it *not* be with such different starting points and assumptions? But Franciscans do not usually fight bishops or diocesan clergy; we are simply concerned with different things. We often fill the gaps with things which are of less interest to them or things for which they have no time. We try to emphasize things like freedom of conscience, joy, creativity, nature, the poor, popular devotion, the view from the edge and the bottom, the "lepers" of society. Just compare Franciscan mission architecture, art, and design in New Mexico, Texas, and California with that of a more European-influenced Midwestern parish. It is a completely different *imaginarium*.

After some of the so-called "Spiritual Franciscans"[6] were burned at the stake in France in 1318 for insisting that Jesus and the apostles were poor and shared all things in common, our order became much more cautious and eager to be verbally orthodox and to fit in with the mainline Church, which was at the height of its temporal power.[7] Heresy had come to be seen as merely *disobedience to authority*, which might well be heresy, but often is not. If Jesus is the primary teacher and reference point for Christianity, then heresy would surely be any lack of love and not just disobedience (notice love is primarily an action called "charity" or kindness). Disobedience is only the primary sin when your primary concern is the maintaining of authority.

But after this early persecution, Franciscans became very eager to be seen as obedient and humble friars, which was, of course, very true to Francis, and did keep us from arrogance. Yet as Peter (the "first pope") said to his own religious authorities: "Obedience to God comes before obedience to men" (Acts 5:29). John the Baptist, Jesus himself, and Paul were all outrageously "disobedient" to their own contemporary religious authorities. How can we miss that? The fact that teachers and priests have ignored this historical fact is a good example of our selective attention and even outright denial. But *you can only see what you are told to pay attention to.* The sad result was that obedience and group loyalty became the primary virtues instead of love or compassion to the outsider. That was still the case when I joined the order in 1961.

BREAKING THE RULES PROPERLY

Nevertheless, it is not wise to fight any large institution or cultural consensus directly because you will seldom win, and you will often become negative and oppositional in the process—and sometimes proud as well. "Every reaction elicits an equal and opposite reaction," as the law of physics tells us. You are better when you just do what you know you must do, and then be willing to pay the price if you are wrong or accused of being wrong. You do much better to quietly go off to the side and do your work, exactly as Francis did in rebuilding San Damiano and the Portiuncula *outside* the walls of Assisi. He respected and honored San Rufino cathedral, San Giorgio school and parish, and San Pietro Monastery *inside* the walls of his hometown, and even made use of their spiritual services, but he went elsewhere to experiment with his "form of life." This is key Third Force strategy, which I will explain shortly.

We Franciscans still to this day humbly pay our yearly basket of fish to the monks at San Pietro to compensate them for the "simple use" of a "Little Portion" of their land outside the city.[8] The notion that we could *use or rent* the land rather than own it was a good compromise and conceit. Not owning property can clearly free you from the power and importance that often come with any notion of mine and thine, and it can allow you your moral high ground if that is what you want. "*Ad Usum Simplicem*," we were told to write in our books as novices. "For the simple use of Friar Richard," I piously printed. I guess I should engrave it on my laptop now!

The centerpiece of those who live an alternative orthodoxy is that they must *learn the rules so well that they know how to break them properly—which, of course, is not really to break them at all.* For example, I often change the wording of many of the official orations of the Catholic Mass, after I find myself praying for my or our own salvation

65 percent of the time (count them yourself). This is not disobedience but, in fact, obedience to the essence of the Gospel itself. It just looks like disobedience to novices, Catholic fundamentalists, and bishops. As Jesus said, "I have not come to abolish the law, but to bring it to perfection or to complete it" (Matthew 5:17).

Paul takes much of the entire book of Romans to clarify this subtle but important distinction between law and faith: "Faith does not make the law pointless, but it does give the law its real value" (Romans 3:31). This is the perennial tension found throughout the Scriptures between the prophetic and the priestly traditions, between denouncing deceit and injustice and still upholding the Tradition. This tension is always necessary, but it is seldom resolved in the Scriptures themselves, except in Jesus and the Jewish prophets. Francis, without doubt, came down on the side of the prophetic without rejecting the priestly, as the whole world seemed to understand by its shock when the new pope did the same and chose his name in 2013. It almost did not seem possible for the ultimate establishment figure to take a very disestablishment name!

THE THIRD FORCE OF THE FRANCISCAN WAY

Francis and Franciscans did not dismiss the priestly tradition, although he himself refused priestly ordination. Francis knew that Jesus said to the newly healed, "Go, show yourself to the priests, as evidence for them" (Luke 17:14). He relied on what might be called Third Force, a

way of responding, without being antagonistic, by introducing alterna-
tives to reframe any issue and create something genuinely new, as the
Holy Spirit always does. The "Law of Three" is dynamic and moving, as
compared to the always oppositional "Law of Two."[9] Francis, without
knowing it, was a teacher of the Third Way, the way of compassionate
creativity, and never got trapped in either fight or flight. [10] Honestly,
that is much of his genius!

You may recall an earlier chapter, where Francis expressed a wish that
the "world would see friars minor very rarely and be filled with wonder
at the smallness of their number."[11] He tried to operate completely
outside any systems of "bigness," and the competition and comparison
that come with it. The idea of progress and growth and being number
one did not yet completely dominate society as it does now. "You are
who you are in the eyes of God, nothing more and nothing less," he
often said.[12] Francis did not see himself as competing with the other
clergy, for or against anyone, but identified with the poorest of the laity
and lived outside of all systems of power. He constantly warned us
against any heady or negative attitudes toward higher-ups.

In the final Rule of 1223, Francis tells the brothers, "Do not criticize
those who wear soft and colorful garments," which is surely a veiled
warning against any judging of the higher clergy and the wealthy.[13] He
also cautions, "Don't be argumentative and take part in disputes with

words, but be courteous and humble." In his final "Testament,"[14] he declares, "I refuse to consider the sins of priests, they are better than I am," and, "We made no claim to learning and were submissive to everyone." The three dangerous and ever-present *P*s of power, prestige, and possessions were of no interest to either Francis or Clare. They both walked confidently, freely, and happily in the other direction. There was no "imitative rivalry" in either of them, which René Girard says is the basis of most human conflict and violence.

Francis's first Rule of 1221, which is really the Franciscans' "foundational document,"[15] was found to be too egalitarian and even naïve by church authorities. In chapter five, Francis said, "All the friars without exception are forbidden to wield power or authority over others." That put them outside the usual systems of domination, clerical authority, or any power seeking. In fact, he was ordered to rewrite this early and idealistic rule (which was largely just Scripture quotes tied together). I admit that much of Jesus's teaching could also be judged naïve, idealistic, or impractical, exactly as the Sermon on the Mount has largely been viewed through most of Christian history. Francis and Clare's approach has been called a "performative spirituality" which means that things are only found to be true *in the doing of them*. At the level of idea, issues will be forever argued about, because thinking is invariably dualistic. Francis wanted us to know things in an almost "cellular" and energetic way, and not just in our heads.

The Franciscan gift is nevertheless to both *reveal and hold* that tension between idealism and actual existence within the Church. We do not resolve such a creative tension by any mental gymnastics or papal dispensation.[16] When you honor both power and powerlessness, you quite simply come up with a third something, a very different kind of power. Third Force activity is invariably the gift of the authentic Gospel for the world, and mystics are Third Force people.

The Franciscan worldview is not heretical, nor is it a threat, except to the comfortable and the careerists. It is not about a struggle for control. If you look at the history of heretics who are condemned, their transgression is normally about issues of authority, priesthood, administration of sacraments, and "Who's got the power?" I cannot think of anyone who was ever burned at the stake for *not* taking care of the widows and orphans, or for any issues of orthopraxy. It is rather shocking when you begin to notice this—after your initial shock in wondering why Christians would ever burn anybody at the stake to begin with! The third shock is that no pope, priest, or parishioner has ever been excommunicated for living too rich a lifestyle, or for being ambitious, greedy, or prideful, even though Jesus condemned these things much more directly and openly than for what we usually excommunicate people.

Jesus does indeed force us toward clear dualistic choices with stories like the camel and the eye of the needle, Lazarus and the rich man, the sheep and the goats, and lines like "You cannot serve both God and money" (Matthew 6:24). It often seems that where Jesus is truly dualistic, we refuse to be, and where Jesus was very unclear or never spoke, we have arrived at absolutely certain conclusions! Check it out for yourself. Organized religion has paid much more attention to some things that Jesus never once mentioned (birth control, abortion, and homosexuality) and rather totally ignores other things that he stated with utter clarity ("Go sell what you have and give it to the poor" [Matthew 19:21]). (I am not trying to be negative, rebellious, or clever, but just trying to name the elephant in the living room that we have all agreed not to notice.

Francis not only named but humbly rode such an elephant in the way he lived his life and the message that his actions clearly conveyed. Francis put almost all of his attention on issues of daily practice, humble relationships, and a way of life rather than on Sunday recitations of creeds. There was nothing to condemn him for and much to admire in this refocusing. He was passionate about different things from what occupied the Church hierarchy; yet he "let sleeping dogs lie," as the saying goes, and did not question orthodox dogmas or liturgical practices (much as Dorothy Day and Oscar Romero did in our own time). Francis and Clare were "fundamentalist" about life practice itself, things that demanded a lot from them personally, and spent almost no

time being fundamentalist about issues that demanded mere conformity from others.

Like all good Catholics, Francis and Clare happily "believed" the
creedal formulations of the Church, and let them hold together the
very psychic structure of their lives and hearts—as the creeds indeed
have the power to do. When you let others worry about the *substructure
and superstructure* of things (that is, about philosophy, church protocols,
and theology), you can put all of your attention on the actual *structure
and practice* of your daily life.

Developing the Franciscan Way after Francis

Very soon after the idyllic first generation of friars, and after Francis
discovered that he could trust *some* intellectuals (he referred to St.
Anthony of Lisbon, later "of Padua," as "my bishop!"), some friars went
off to university settings, especially Paris and Oxford, probably as lay
preachers, and perhaps to gather some of the young educated men into
the fledgling and largely uneducated community. In the next generation of Franciscans were names like Alexander of Hales, William
of Ockham, Roger Bacon, Adam Marsh, John Duns Scotus, John
Peckham (a later archbishop of Canterbury), Raymond Lull, and especially Bonaventure of Bagnoregio.

In their own unique way, and now with intellectual gifts, they
continued to develop the themes of a truly alternative orthodoxy. In

some ways, this alternative attitude is crystalized in Bonaventure's famous "Defense of the Mendicants" debate at Paris, where the friars were clearly seen as doing theology and ministry differently from the other orders or from previous academics. The new mendicant ("begging") orders were receiving a lot of criticism and push back from the secular clergy and the academy at that time, because they did not follow the old rules of intellectual argument or treat the academy itself as home base. The basis and even authority for our ministry was not the parish structure as much as it was living in a para-church community and close to the marginalized.

Franciscans, however, were usually not the winners of these intellectual debates with the more educated Dominicans; we invariably held the minority position—which was not condemned but merely deemed "a minority position." It was sort of like the dissenting side of an American Supreme Court decision or the way that scientists work with a hypothesis until it is formally disproven.[17] In some ways, the Western Church did not become so totally dualistic in its thinking until after the Reformation and the rational Enlightenment. After the printing press, words became more important than actual experience.

HETERODOXY

A heterodox opinion is what we would now call a minority opinion. It is not deemed wrong or heretical or rebellious as such, but is simply not the mainstream thought. In that clear sense, Franciscanism has invariably been heterodox, but we usually kept that quiet, just knew it from the inside, and went about our business.

So any debates about Franciscan spirituality were not usually oppositional but had to do with *what* was stressed and *how* it was stressed, which makes a lot of difference in your practical ethos and imaginal world. What you stress and how you stress it determine what you pay attention to and what you are allowed to ignore. Most groups actually operate this way without admitting it. In general, we taught that love and action were more important than intellect or speculative truth. Love is the highest category for the Franciscan School (the goal), and we believe that authentic love is not possible without true inner freedom of conscience,[18] nor will love be real or tested unless we somehow live close to the disadvantaged (its method), who remind us about what is important.

Good Franciscan spirituality always tries to maintain three freedoms all at once:

First, God's freedom to do what God wills, even when it is beyond our understanding (God does not need to follow our rules, and God's will is always finally a mystery).

Second, the maintenance of structural freedom wherever possible.

Third, some form of contemplative prayer is the way to maintain that inner, psychological freedom—so we can do the first two.

Such an immense sky of freedom is a big and scary order, and probably few achieve it, but it is still the clear ideal (Galatians 5:1ff.). Freedom is not a bad word in Franciscan spirituality, as long as it is not just the kind of egocentric and individualistic freedom we have in the West today.

This love of inner freedom surely relegated Franciscans to a position suspect by the hierarchy, but it also made us much more accepting of human failure and individual conscience among ordinary believers. As a confessor, I was trained by some holy friars not to sit on a judgment seat, but only and forever on the "mercy seat" when I was listening to people's stories. As the book of Exodus says of the mercy seat above the Ark of the Covenant, "There I shall come to meet you" (25:22). No wonder people like to go to Franciscans for confession!

So on two levels, in our emphasis on orthopraxy (simplicity, nonviolence, living among the poor, love of creation) and in our thought (a nonviolent atonement theory, univocity of all being, freedom of conscience, contemplative prayer), we Franciscans found ourselves indeed brothers in the minority class and "poor daughters" of Clare on the invisible edge of the Church, which is exactly where Francis wanted us to be and surely how Clare and he radically lived.

It is only in the late twentieth and early twenty-first centuries that we find this alternative orthodoxy again being rediscovered, honored, and recognized as perhaps the more important shape of and witness to orthodoxy itself. As Pope Paul VI said, "The world will no longer believe teachers unless they are first of all witnesses."[19]

Francis and Clare were such witnesses for us, Bonaventure, Scotus, and others were the teachers, and even today we are trying to be both living witnesses and good teachers in our eagerness to love.[20] Let me end this chapter with an attempt at a summary of our heterodoxy:

First, there must be the living,
Which must lead to a giving,
Then you realize you do not yet know love!
So you re-enter the circle of living and giving.
You make steps backward,
While wanting to go forward.
(And you actually do go forward—but secretly!)
If you stay inside this circle,
It eventually creates one human life,
Which can never happen just inside the mind
(We might call this a "virtuous circle").
There is no straight line to Goodness, to Love, or to God.
And thank God,
Grace is always retroactive.

CHAPTER SEVEN

The Franciscan Genius:
The Integration of the Negative

You can show your love to others by *not* wishing that they should be better Christians.[1]

—Francis of Assisi

We must bear patiently *not* being good...and *not* being thought good.[2]

—Francis of Assisi

Yes, you read the quotes above correctly. The first quote was considered so untrue, so impossible that Francis would write such a thing, that for centuries we deleted the "not" in the text! In the second quote, the point seems to have largely been ignored or denied until the very same thing was taught by a later female doctor of the Church, St. Thérèse of Lisieux, in the nineteenth century. Maybe you would have automatically deleted the "nots" yourself, as I would have, which is why I italicized them.

Why *were* those "nots" deleted? I think that the piously corrected versions provided us with an illusion about our own superiority that very much appeals to the ego, especially the religious ego. Francis's statements come from a highly enlightened awareness, honest self-observation, and the humility that always comes with it.

I suppose there is no more counterintuitive spiritual idea than the possibility that God might actually *use and find necessary* what we fear, avoid, deny, and deem unworthy. This is what I mean by the "integration of the negative." Yet I believe this is the core of Jesus's revolutionary Good News, Paul's deep experience, and the central insight that Francis and Clare lived out with such simple elegance. The integration of the negative still has the power to create "people who are turning the whole world upside down" (Acts 17:6), as was said of the early Christians gathered at Jason's house. Now some therapists call this pattern "embracing your shadow," which makes it into a "golden shadow" in its gifts to us. Such *surrendering of superiority, or even a need for such superiority,* is central to any authentic enlightenment. Without it, we are blind ourselves (John 9:39–41) and blind guides for others.

An Inherent Asymmetry

Francis and Clare made what most would call *negative or disadvantage* shimmer and shine by their delight in what the rest of us ordinarily oppose, deny, and fear: things like being small, poor, disparaged, being outside the system of power and status, weakness in any form, or what Francis generally referred to as *minoritas*. This is a different world than most of us choose to live in. We all seem invariably to want to join in the "majority" and the admired.[3] Francis and Clare instead make a preemptive strike at both life and death, offering a voluntary assent to Full Reality in all its tragic wonder. They make a loving bow to the very things that defeat, scare, and embitter most of the rest of us. You might call it "dying before you die," which is always the secret of the saints, and the heart of any authentic spiritual initiation.[4]

We now know from astrophysics that the universe was born in perfect temperature, balance, and symmetry at the time of the Big Bang, but it was only as we cooled into *asymmetry* that the very forces of the world changed so that life—and eventually human life—could exist at all! *We now live because of disorder and imperfection, and totally inside of an asymmetrical universe—which is itself a new kind of symmetry.*[5] According to modern physics, the whole universe knows how to incorporate the would-be "problem," the seeming negative (electrons must balance protons in the atom), and then make it into a larger life, as does much of modern philosophy and psychology too.

Critical or "negative" thinking has led us to an honesty about words and truth that we now call postmodernism. It can make us totally cynical or allow us to be ready for mature faith like never before. Facing our shadow self and our addictions is almost the heart of modern psychiatry and therapy. Religion had best catch up with the other disciplines and relearn the absolute centrality of what should have been its own original message.

Unfortunately, the Christian metaphor for the negative side became "carrying our cross" and, as valid as that is, our glib misuse of it and our fear of "self negation" has made most people unable to hear the word "cross" in any helpful way. I personally think that honesty about ourselves and all of reality is the way that God made grace totally free and universally available, because we all find our lives eventually dragged into opposition, problems, "the negative" (sin, failure, betrayal, gossip, fear, hurt, disease, etc.), and especially the ultimate negation: death itself. Good spirituality should utterly prepare us for that, instead of teaching us high-level denial or pretense.

Any ladder to climb only appeals to our egotistic consciousness, and our need to *win or be right,* which is not really holiness at all—although it has been a common counterfeit for holiness in much of Christian history. In the Franciscan reading of the Gospel there is no reason to be religious or to love God except "to love much the one who has loved us much," as Francis said.[6] The Ten Commandments are about creating social order (a good thing), but the eight Beatitudes (Matthew 5:3–12) of Jesus are all about *incorporating what seems like disorder,* which is much better. But no county or city, to my knowledge, has put a monument to the eight Beatitudes on their courthouse lawn. These are two very different levels of consciousness.

Franciscan spirituality almost entirely proceeds from a spirituality of the Beatitudes. With the Beatitudes, there is no social or ego payoff for the false self, whereas obedience to the Ten Commandments does give us the necessary impulse control and containment we need to get started, which is a foundational need in the first half of life.[7] Both "halves of life" are good and necessary, but the Ten Commandments are more oriented toward the tasks of the first half of life. "I have kept all these from my youth," the rich young man says, while he then refuses to go further (Mark 10:22). The Beatitudes, however, reveal a world of pure grace and abundance, or what Spiral Dynamics or Integral Theory would call the third tier of consciousness or non-dual thinking and what I would call second-half-of-life spirituality.[8] Healthy religion is "made to order" to send you through your entire life journey and not just offer you containment.

In a world where imperfection seems to be everywhere, the humble and honest have a huge head start in spiritual matters, and can first and always find God in their simple lives. "To the poor in spirit the kingdom of heaven belongs" (Matthew 5:3), as Jesus puts it in the first line of the Sermon on the Mount. And Mary says the same in her proclamation of the Magnificat: "The proud are cast down from their thrones and the lowly will be lifted up" (Luke 1:52). But the ego so hates and resists this truth that it can only come to us as "a word from God" or a word from beyond.

Less than one percent of humanity since the beginning of time has had access to church, sacraments, trained ministers, formal religious education, the Bible, or even reading itself. That does and should tell us something. The only thing we all have in common is that we all "sin," transgress, fall into imperfection, and fail (Romans 5:12). We are also *sinned against* as the victims of others' failure and the social milieu. Augustine called this inherited wound "original sin."

In *a spirituality of imperfection*, we have a universal basis for how God "saves" humanity, and perhaps also a clear naming of what God saves us from—which is mainly from ourselves and our own hated "unworthiness," plus the unworthiness of others. One of the most helpful pieces of advice I ever got from Francis is in the seventh chapter of our Rule, where he tells us not to be upset because of the sins or mistakes of others "because such anger or annoyance will make it difficult to be charitable."[9] His analysis is that simple, that hard, and that true, and it puts the onus all back on me. I have had to reread that quote many times.

Unworthiness Is the Ticket

Entering the spiritual search for truth and for ourselves through the so-called negative, or what seems like the back door, takes all elitism out of spirituality, which is its most common temptation. Now the usual claims which appeal to our ego self ("I am an advanced person") are of no use whatsoever and are actually revealed as much of the problem. It makes arrogant religion largely impossible and reveals any violent religion as an oxymoron (although that has sadly not been the case up to now). In this negative frame, the quickest ticket to heaven, enlightenment, or salvation is "unworthiness" itself, or at least a willingness to face our own smallness and incapacity. Our conscious need for mercy is our only real boarding pass. *The ego does not like that very much, but the soul fully understands.*

Probably no group has made this message more practical and more obvious than the modern twelve-step recovery movement.[10] "Hi, I'm Joe, and I am an alcoholic" is a very honest way to start a spiritual meeting. Maybe that is why it works for so many. We also start our Catholic liturgy with three recitations of "Lord, have mercy" and later with "Lord, I am not worthy to receive you"—but we then move ahead as if that were not true, and quickly presume we are indeed "worthy" to receive communion, and others are supposedly unworthy or do not understand as perfectly as we do. Do any Catholics even begin to *understand* what they are doing? Yet anyone else, outside the "fully understanding" Catholic circle, is told not to participate. This is one of the most visible and really tragic results of a spirituality of supposed "perfection." Such exclusionary tactics are unconsciously based on a false sense of our own worthiness and then faith is treated as if it were memorized knowledge.

THE IDEA OF RELIGION

I read years ago that *the idea of religion began with the making of a simple but fatal distinction*: in different ways, humans falsely divide the world into the pure and the impure, the totally good and the totally bad, the perfect and the imperfect. It starts with such totally dualistic thinking and then is never able to get beyond it. Such a total split or clean division is never true in actual experience—we all know that reality is a lot more mixed and "disordered" than that. You have to really close down to continue to see things in such a false way. Immature religion then moves from this *first false assumption* toward an entire ethical code, a priesthood of some sort, and various rituals and taboos to keep us on the side of the seeming pure, positive, perfect, and good—as if that were even possible. Didn't you ever wonder why Jesus refused to wash his hands, as was required (Matthew 15:2)? Such a system sounds right, but it never entirely works except in the mind—and even then it demands denial, splitting, and mental pretense. All religion, without actual God experience, remains immature and largely self-referential. How could it not be? God, however, forgives even immature religion, and those who know God learn to do the same.

I mean this next point kindly, but organized religion is almost structurally certain to create *hypocrites* (literally meaning "actors"), those who try to *appear* to be pure and good, or at least better than others. Who of us doesn't want that? Jesus uses the word at least ten times in Matthew's Gospel alone. This tendency toward hypocrisy is a largely structural problem, one you can expect to find in all idealistic and spiritual groups, where we are unconsciously trained to want to look good, to seek moral high ground, to split, and see the "speck" in other people's eyes and not see the "log" in our own. None of us lives up to all of our spoken ideals, but we have to pretend that we do to feel good about ourselves and to get others of our chosen group to respect us. (Note how Francis brilliantly counters that in the epigraphs that begin this chapter.)

Any *top-down religion* trains you in pretending, denying, and projecting your evil elsewhere, without wanting you to realize that you are doing this. It is surely why Jesus emphasizes inner experience ("going into the desert") over Temple worship ("outer formalities"), although he does not throw out the second either (he is a non-dual thinker). Yet this pretending and projecting of our evil elsewhere is precisely why external religion is so very dangerous and how it enables and protects such a high number of immature laity and clergy—who are able to think they are much more loving and proper than they really are.

Honest self-knowledge, shadow work, therapy, and tools like the Enneagram are dismissed with such hostility by many fervent believers that you know they are hiding something or afraid of something. They disdain this work as "mere psychology." If so, then the desert fathers and mothers, the *Philokalia*, Thomas Aquinas and Teresa of Ávila, were already into "mere psychology," as was Jesus. Without a very clear struggle with our shadow self and some form of humble and honest confession of our imperfections, none of us can or will face our own hypocrisy. This needed work is indeed "spiritual warfare," as the desert monks called it, since it takes conscious and sustained struggle to be aware of the shadow self—which only takes ever more subtle disguises the "holier" you get.

THE LITTLE WAY OF WEAKNESS

God's "immoral minority," so to speak, tries to incorporate, choose, and even seek out what Paul taught as his doctrine of the cross: *"I am glad for weaknesses, constraints, and distress for Christ's sake, for it is when I am weak that I am strong"* (2 Corinthians 12:10). He reported that Christ had said to him, "My grace is sufficient for you; for my strength is made perfect in weakness" (2 Corinthians 12:9), just as Jesus was *first resurrected already on the cross.* Chained in his jail cell, Paul writes to the Philippians and dares to say to them, "What I once considered an asset I now consider a disadvantage" (Philippians 3:7). Paul, following Jesus, has forever reversed the engines of ego and its attainments, and it is this precise reversal of values—and new entrance point—that Francis and Clare understood so courageously and clearly. St. Thérèse of Lisieux (1873–1897), a Carmelite nun who became the youngest, least educated, and most quickly made doctor of the Church, also sought this downward path, which she called "a new way" or her "little way." But it took seven more centuries to get there.

Thérèse was right on both counts, since her way of life was indeed very new for most people and very "little" instead of the usual upward-bound Christian agenda; "to do little things with great love" was the goal for Thérèse.[11] Most Catholics lovingly call her "The Little Flower," perhaps the only saint whose nickname dominates her real name. The mainline path of most Christianity by her time had become largely perfectionistic and legalistic, making the good news anything but good or inviting for generations of Catholics and Christians.[12]

Thérèse, almost counter to reason, says: *"Whoever is willing to serenely bear the trial of being displeasing to herself, that person is a pleasant place of shelter for Jesus."*[13] If you observe yourself, you will see how hard it is to be "displeasing" to yourself, and that is the initial emotional snag that sends most of us into terribly bad moods without even realizing the origins of the mood. So to resolve this common problem, both Francis and Thérèse teach us to let go of the very need to "think well of yourself" to begin with! That is your ego talking, not God, they would say. Only someone who has surrendered their foundational egocentricity can do this, of course. Psychiatrist and popular writer in the 1980s Scott Peck told me personally over lunch that this quote was "sheer religious genius" on her part, because it made the usual posturing of religion well-nigh impossible. It mirrors what Francis said in the epigraphs to this chapter.

I am afraid most early religious training is about the "big way" instead of Thérèse's "little way." In some cases, seminaries, novitiates, and even Sunday sermons became professional and high-level training in what is called "Pharisaism" or public posing and pretending—largely without realizing that this is what they are doing. I do not believe that is an exaggeration; the constancy of this problem is revealed by Jesus's strongest words in the Gospels (most of Matthew 23 takes your breath away with its anger at religion and hypocrisy).

Pharisaism can only work if your religion keeps you "unconscious" and on cultural cruise control. Such immature religion is almost always preoccupied with externals, formulas, exact rituals performed exactly, costumes, roles, and titles—and obedience and group loyalty as the highest virtues instead of love. Proudly wearing my brown and corded Franciscan habit for more than fifty years now, I know it is very dangerous to "dress up," both for me and for those who relate to me so differently when I am wearing it. Ironically, the Gospel and Francis are about "dressing down." Francis dressed down to look poor, and now we Franciscans dress up to look like him!

When you have not had any internal experience of God and grace, you almost always overcompensate with external window dressing. The "window dressings" are not wrong in themselves, but do tend to make *nonessentials into the essentials that we obsess about and divide over.* When you have done this for half of your life, it is very hard to let go of it. But many do it quite naturally. I remember one humble oblate bishop in the Yukon who told me that every time he had to put on his "silly hat" it was like being crowned with thorns! Only authentic God experience, along with some kind of "falling," could have accomplished this radical surgery of his ego needs.[14] I heard of another bishop who wanted to be buried in his mitre, however. *You never become humble except through fully accepting humiliations—usually many times.*

Sometimes, I have felt like Paul must have felt when he shouted to his newly liberated converts, who were still looking to the law for their salvation, "You stupid Galatians! After having such a clear picture of the crucified, who has put this spell on you?... You began in the Spirit and you are ending in the flesh!" (Galatians 3:1, 3). Most of us begin with lessons and laws, and then we stay there forever; we never make it to the Spirit. It is a kind of stalling in the first half of our lives, even though Paul made it quite clear that *"If you are guided by the Spirit, you are not under the law"* (Galatians 5:18). I know such a line must be scary because it feels as if there are no guidelines now (I would be called a heretic if I said it without quoting Paul); but until we discover the "little way," we almost all try to gain moral high ground by obeying laws and thinking we are thus spiritually advanced. Yet Thérèse said, *"It is enough to recognize one's nothingness and to abandon oneself, like a child, into God's arms."*[15] People who follow this more honest path are invariably more joyful, more compassionate, and have plenty of time for simple gratitude about everything. They do not need mitres of any sort.

WAITING FOR GOD'S "MORE"

In terms of spirituality, as in good art, *less is usually more.* Or, to put it another way, small is beautiful. Only by continually choosing a philosophy of "less" that is willing to wait for God's "more," will we grow and transform, since we have then learned to be taught by smallness and ordinariness. We will practically experience this as *a growth in willingness and a surrendering of willfulness.* This is another aspect of incorporating the negative, which then ends up not being negative at all but just a positive appreciation for *what is.*

This gospel reversing of engines is undoubtedly more necessary than ever for those of us raised in a Western culture of climbing, competing, and comparing—where there is no room for falling, for less, or for delight in the ordinary. Our poor young people want to be on the stage of *American Idol, America's Got Talent,* and *Dancing with the Stars.* And every year, it seems that our restaurants, our parties, our cars, and our tastes have to be one step higher, better, and beyond last year's.[16] This is surely not a program for happiness, because such constant expectation breeds deep discontent. It is no wonder that half of our country feels so ready to be angry or offended much of the time.

I hope you now see more clearly how Francis cannot be written off as a mere soft and sweet figure. Looking clearly at his actual life and practice shows how *he was deliberately and consciously undercutting the entire "honor/shame system" on which so much of culture, violence, false self-esteem, and even many of the ministrations of church totally depend.*[17] Doing anything and everything *purely for God* is certainly the most purifying plan for happiness I can imagine. It changes the entire nature of human interaction and eliminates most conflict.

When Francis said that he had to wear patches on the outside of his habit to show what he was like on the inside, when he walked through Assisi in his underwear and played seesaw in the piazza when he heard he was being called a saint, we know we are dealing with a person who has moved beyond the world that most of us inhabit. He rebuilt the spiritual life on "love alone," and let go of the lower-level needs of social esteem, security, self-image, and manufacturing of persona. Remember, *when your only goal is love, especially love of God, you really cannot fail.* And that is really true!

Now that you know this about Francis, I hope you will have the courage to see that this message of simplicity, smallness, and "downward mobility" is rather clear in the Christian Scriptures too (Philippians 2:7; 2 Corinthians 8:9; for example). I also hope you will not just believe it because I said it (because then you will forget it). Most saints lived such simplicity without usually being able to verbalize why it was the true and natural way to live. Mother Elizabeth Seton put it so clearly: "Let's live simply so others can simply live."[18] Accepting the entire path of littleness, within and without, might well be the only way we can practically survive together on this planet in the next centuries.

Let me end with an almost perfect Franciscan poem by a modern and wise poet, Chris Ellery, written in honor of John the Baptist. I am honored that he gave me permission to use this as-yet-unpublished poem. His lovely metaphor for our humble returning to the Source, like John the Baptist wanting to get smaller, is simply the natural descent and ready evaporation of water itself. No wonder that Francis called her "Sister Water, so useful, lowly, precious, and fair!" Water always and forever seeks the lower, and even the lowest, place. We must let water be our teacher here. And water, as you know, is the one single universal element necessary for all of life. Teresa of Avila felt that water in all its qualities and movements was the most perfect metaphor for the entire spiritual journey. I would agree with her.

> When I fear I have done wrong,
> when I look to those who are less than wise,
> when I forget transcendence and kneel in the meanings of
>   color and shadow,
> when I tell lies to my soul,
> I seek out water, I follow its charm—a river, a stream,
> a lake with its springs and currents.
> See how it offers life
> as it flawlessly flows and forms
> to the shape of this world, the contours of land, the urge of
>   earth,
> hear how it sings under the sun
> of endless evaporation.[19]

Lightness of Heart and Firmness of Foot: The Integration of Feminine and Masculine

We two being one, are it![1]

—JOHN DONNE

I ALWAYS KNEW THAT THE Franciscans were on a rather different track than the monastic or other male orders in the Roman Catholic Church, but it took me a long time to articulate why this floating intuition was true. Franciscans are not better or worse than the others, just clearly different. The basis of my intuition, and the actual difference, has to do in part, I believe, with the integration of the feminine. One scholar rightly says that Francis "without having a specific feminist program... contributed to the feminizing of Christianity."[2] French historian André Vauchez, in his critical biography of Francis, adds that this integration of the feminine "constitutes a fundamental turning point in the history of Western spirituality."[3] I think they are both onto something, which creates the distinctiveness and even the heart of the Franciscan way.

Clare is clearly the Franciscans' archetypal symbol of the feminine, and Francis almost supernaturally exemplifies it—and even "gets away with it." In my view, Franciscanism was originally integrating the feminine element into a very patriarchal and overly masculinized Roman Church, and also into a somewhat harsh male spirituality of the desert, and even into an overscheduled spirituality in the monasteries. Franciscanism integrated the feminine first of all on the level of imagination (see chapter sixteen), but also through some very different emphases, new names for roles and functions, and rather new familial structures. (For example, we do not operate as a hierarchy, but make our decisions communally in chapters, and every assignment I have ever been given was made in full consultation with me personally. Francis also forbad us to use any titles implying up and down, like prior, abbot, or superior.)

When I say "feminine" and "masculine," what in the East might be referred to as yin and yang, I am defining these categories, based on my observation and study, in these general ways.[4] The feminine principle has greater interest in the inner, the soul, the formless, deeper feeling, intuition, connections, harmony, beauty, and relationality in general; it is more identified with lunar subtlety and not the over-differentiating light of the masculine sun god or the literalism and linearity of the left brain. Not all women fully identify with the feminine principle, of course, and some men do, but these descriptors give you a sense of what I mean by the feminine. Karl Jung calls it a more "diffused awareness," both for good and for ill.

The masculine principle, as I experience it and have taught it, is more interested in the outer, the mental, the form, the idea, the movement or action of things, the naming and differentiation of things one from another; separate solar clarity, as it were, as opposed to the relationship of one thing to another. It prefers the ascent of spirit and mind to the descent of soul. It often moves toward "agency" and action before relationship or intimacy. Just watch little boys play, and watch men construct and demolish. I think I have earned the right to say this after twenty-five years of men's work and retreats in many cultures. It is often a more "focused awareness," both for good and for ill.

The masculine principle is exactly what we see in Adam before the creation of Eve, as he *names and differentiates* each thing. This was a solitary kind of knowing, before his necessary helpmate joined him and brought a different and complementary way of being. Then note that one of the first things said about Eve when she is created is that she is both "naked" and "without shame" (Genesis 2:25), which is a rather fine statement of feminine vulnerability and perception. At this point, Adam shares in that nakedness and lack of shame, but perhaps has only come to this awareness in his new relatedness with his counterpart, Eve.

Even more wonderfully, the first statement made about Yahweh God after Adam and Eve both fall into shame is that "God sews clothes for them out of hides with which they covered themselves" (Genesis 3:21). So the first metaphor we have for God—after Creator itself—is a "maternal" seamstress who takes away human shame. It is as if Yahweh God makes male and female *mutuality* possible and attractive by telling them they do not need to be afraid of one another or themselves—or "him" [*sic*]. The Great God who meets the people of Israel is a protector and a reconciler of opposites, in this case of maleness and femaleness itself.

Gender, and the dance of gender, seems to be a foundational opposition in the human mind, which is why many languages (but not English) even speak of words and things as masculine or feminine. Our deep preoccupation with gender also helps explain why gender taboos (LGBT issues) are often the very last and hardest to be resolved, even among people who consider themselves quite open and progressive. Gender seems to be a very deep archetype in the soul, and thus any gender identity confusion is indeed quite confusing as long as the mind is still trapped in dualisms, or as long as we still try to read reality in a non-contemplative or egoic way.

LIGHTNESS OF HEART AND FIRMNESS OF FOOT

I have often sensed this different path with regard to the masculine and feminine principles in many of the Franciscan Sisters and Secular

Franciscans that I have met and worked with over the years. They were not any better than Sisters of Mercy or Sisters of Charity, nor any better than Carmelites or Salesians. In fact, part of their Franciscan giveaway was that they did not need to be better or considered better! Yet they were clearly standing on a different ground and foundation. The best I can do in trying to describe this more feminine ground would be in this way: Happy and healthy Franciscans seem to present *a combination of lightness of heart and firmness of foot at the same time.* By this I mean that they do not take themselves so seriously, as upward-bound men often do; yet they do what they do with quiet conviction and full purpose as mature women often do.

I see this synthesis of both lightness and firmness as a more "feminine" approach to spirituality, and I surely see it beautifully exemplified in both Clare and Francis in different ways. It is a rare combination, so much so that it might be seen as a kind of holy foolishness in both of them. Androgyny is invariably a threatening Third Force if we are over-identified with one side or the other.

Clare asks from the papacy that she be allowed to found her community on her privately conceived and untested ground that she calls her "privilege of poverty." Then she waits patiently on her deathbed for the papal bull to arrive, knowing it will; but there is no evidence of her demanding, whining, or wrangling with prelates or theology beforehand. She quietly knows she will win, even though there is no precedent for women without dowries or patrons being able to sustain themselves.

As to Francis, he twirls around like a top at a crossroads to discern which way God wants him to go, and then sets off with utter confidence in the direction where he finally lands (which would drive a Jesuit crazy). Neither of these ways are classic Catholic means of discernment, decision-making, or discovering God's will. *But I believe the lightness of heart comes from contact with deep feminine intuition and with consciousness itself; the firmness of foot emerges when that feminine principle integrates with the mature masculine soul and moves forward with confidence into the outer world.*

Two Ways of Knowing Reality

Two books in particular helped me name this difference and support my own lived intuitions: Karl Stern's *The Flight from Woman*, which I read in college (around 1965), and Leonardo Boff's *St. Francis: A Model for Human Liberation*. Stern contrasts Francis with the French existentialist Jean-Paul Sartre to illustrate two very different ways of knowing reality. He interestingly calls the masculine way "the Way of the Dynamo" (productivity, rationality, critical thinking, and effectiveness), exemplified by Sartre. And he calls the feminine way "the Way of the Virgin" (relationality, subtlety, and interiority). Francis, he says, exemplified the way of the Virgin, and was in love with "matter and the maternal," whereas Sartre was cynical about almost everything and was estranged "from matter and the maternal that reached a point of no return"; he "turned from the breast of nature in disgust" toward his own critical mind.[5] Francis, by contrast, was totally at home in nature and could experience reality by other means than the mere thinking mind.

You might call Sartre and much Western philosophy "excarnational," whereas Francis was fully and happily *incarnational*, through his falling in love with Jesus and all of creation. (Psychologically speaking, for a heterosexual male to fall in ecstatic love with Jesus, he *must* be in touch with his feminine soul.) My sense is that much of the Roman Church and its clergy reflect a more masculine way of knowing and relating. Catholics constantly say that our honoring of Mary the virgin shows how we love the feminine, but then we grant little or no authority to actual women in decision-making or leadership. In doing so the Roman Church rejects Christianity's incarnational grounding in the nature of things and creation itself, and apes instead the cultural and juridical systems of Western monarchies. Incarnation is not a "liberal" idea, but one mirrored in the whole universe.[6]

Note the simplicity and utter clarity of the way the Jewish Jesus uses common metaphors like red sky, donkey in a ditch, lily in the field, hen and chicks, as well as parabolic storytelling, to make major theological points. Yet these would be considered lightweight arguments, "mere anecdotes," in most seminary and Catholic circles to this day. I would say that Jesus himself represents a more feminine way of knowing and teaching, which we will also see in Francis, who is most effective when he is anecdotal and "presentational" in his message. (He was a master at what we would now call guerrilla or street theater.)

God's eternal self-revelation to creation cannot possibly depend on being academic, much less arguing in a certain Western philosophical way that has been practiced almost exclusively by males until our time. God, as Paul said, "is not far from any of us, since it is in him that we live, and move, and have our being. So that all nations might seek the Divine, and *by feeling their way toward him*, succeed in finding him" (Acts 17:27–28). How did we lose such common-sense wisdom? It is sad indeed that this teaching about intuition and timing has not been more studied and honored, so that our people were allowed to "feel their way toward God." It seems we have too often favored the mind over the heart, the rational over the intuitive, or if you will, the masculine over the feminine.

THE TRIUMPH OF *LOGOS* OVER *EROS*

In his biography of Francis, Leonardo Boff says much the same but with a different vocabulary.[7] He calls the Western preference for the masculine principle the triumph of *logos* over *ethos* or *eros*; a kind of in-house logic that only fully makes sense inside of its own closed system; a love of order in itself; a kind of practical aggressiveness, which soon becomes its own kind of irrationality but is well hidden behind its agreed-upon but untested assumptions. Most of the operations of legislatures and congresses reveal this form of reasoning and debate. It is invariably based on assertions that are usually advantageous to those who are in power (such as trickle-down economics), but spoken with such certitude that the ordinary person assumes such people must be smart and have totally educated opinions. (An obvious church example of the same is that all of the official "seven sacraments" just happen to make us totally dependent upon the priestly class for "grace," and make unmediated contact with God appear to be less likely or not even possible.) Such "patriarchy" makes everybody lose, even the patriarchs themselves because they lose their deep honesty and their feminine souls.

This preference for control over relationship ends up making *dominative power the primary response to most problems of life*, as we saw for example in the Crusades, the Inquisition, the conquest of the New World, Christian support for almost all wars, and clergy sexual abuse (and the bishops' response to it). This seems to be what happens in every culture I know of, when the feminine principle is not introduced, honored, and incorporated. The only known example of Jesus's use of dominative power is against the religious and economic structure of the Temple itself, when he symbolically "cleanses" it, which itself reveals his preference for people and animals over structures, most especially self-serving religious structures.

FEMININE INTERIOR FREEDOM AND SPIRITUALITY

Clare holds the feminine principle, both in her person and also "in place," in fact a very concrete place, the little monastery of San Damiano outside the walls of Assisi, and outside any previous pattern of feminine religious life. We must know the deep significance of what she demanded from the papacy—her "privilege of poverty"—which kept her outside all ecclesiastical systems of control through stipends, dowries, foundations, and subsidies from bishops, relatives, patrons, or rich donors. She kept her freedom. She intentionally chose a defense-less position, rightly recognizing that money distorts and controls almost everything. This is a strong and feminine spirituality that says *I can do what I must do without all your protection, your money, and the control that comes with patronage.*

Clare, and other women like Hildegard of Bingen before her in the twelfth century and Julian of Norwich after her in the fourteenth century, moved Christian spirituality toward interior motivation and intentionality, toward concrete techniques for inner peace and joy, and toward a strong inner sense of the self-in-God. Her canonization as a saint shortly after her death signaled a move toward recognizing *living stories of actually transformed people* and not just stories of strong willpower, enforcers of morality, holders of church offices, or heroic martyrdom that characterized most saints up to that time. *Odium Fidei* ("hatred of the faith") is still sufficient cause for a martyr's canonization, which really says nothing necessarily about the person killed as much as the hate-filled person who killed them.

The first Franciscan martyrs, in Morocco in 1220, seem to have gone there precisely to get martyred! I'm not sure that is holiness as such, but rather a "false masculine" form of spirituality. Maybe that is why, according to Jordan of Giano, Francis ordered the friars not to talk about the Moroccan martyrs, nor to read glorious accounts of their martyrdom, but instead to concentrate on their own necessary sufferings,[8] which again shows his subtle spiritual genius. We do have accounts of a deep transformation of consciousness in Paul and Augustine's writings, but not many others among early saints. The "inner world" was not of interest to most people until the very modern period. Important history happened in the outer world of action and power. When I first studied history, it was mostly a chronicle of who killed whom and who won!

Francis did not waste time in moral or mental gymnastics to assert that he, or his group, was right or superior. As we have seen, Francis would be quite content for his "friars minor" not to be very visible at all. (As noted in chapter six, perhaps we should remind vocational recruiters of this quote.) How utterly different from the usual performance principle that we expect in the male-dominated world. It shows Francis manifesting a very non-male response concerning size, quantity, speed, productivity, and effectiveness, which men for some reason tend to ape and idealize. (And many modern women have joined them, to be quite honest.)

Francis seemed more concerned about "giving his flesh for the life of the world" (John 6:51), as a mother gives her breast to her child (Isaiah 49:15), or a hen covers her chicks with her wings (Luke 13:34), to use Jesus's own feminine metaphor. Francis himself says in chapter six of the Rule that "Just as a mother loves and cares for her child in the flesh, a friar should love and care for his brother in the spirit all the more tenderly." He himself seems to love and use images of nurturance and healing throughout his writings.

The Wounds Left by Patriarchy

Francis's perspective is all the more remarkable when you know all that he had to overcome in his thirteenth-century patriarchal society.[9] By patriarchy ("the rule of the fathers"), I mean when any group or individual operates in such a way that others *must concede so that the dominant group is always first, in control, and right.* Patriarchy frames life as essentially *competition* and "the survival of the fittest," and there must be clear winners and losers. This is an obvious case of the dualistic mind at work, I think. And, of course, women can be matriarchs and dualistic too.

Maybe we can only recognize the character of patriarchy by meeting its opposite—people and structures that are *not* that way. A rather revealing example of either patriarchal or maternal worldviews is revealed in how each perspective differently understands "table fellowship." The meal for both Jesus and Francis was maternal, and by that I mean that it *included, fed, and healed, and never excluded, identified, or punished.* Check it out for yourself. Jesus even accepted and blessed a woman's presence at a male-only meal (Luke 7:36–50), and Francis did the same with Lady Jacoba, who was allowed to enter the friary and even attend his death there.

How many stories do we have of Jesus "multiplying food" in which abundance and leftovers are always mentioned? His meals are never for a few or for the elite. Francis's life has frequent stories of eating with the group, with the people, with Clare, with the sick, with Muslims, and with those who were too weak to fast. Eating was a social event that included and created community for both Jesus and Francis, and there is no indication it was ever a reward for good behavior or an attempt to give a group its separate or superior identity. Can you even imagine Jesus making sure there were no Samaritans or Syro-Phoenicians eating his multiplied food?

Yet a sustained patriarchal worldview has succeeded in using our central holy meal of Eucharist itself to *exclude and judge* the supposedly unworthy (as if we who participate are worthy), to restrict it to those who understand (as if any of us do), and to maintain proper group membership (yet Jesus feeds Judas, who is about to betray him, and Peter, who will deny him). All of these exclusionary restrictions seem to make the Eucharist something less than a truly holy meal, and they only make sense to someone seeking control of the group. Immature maleness even uses Sacraments to control and define its group instead of to heal and feed the thousands as Jesus did.[10] As Pope Francis says, the Eucharist is not a "prize for the perfect."

I use this example of table fellowship because it continues to wound many people and falsely exalt other people. It is a sad instance of overly masculinized spirituality that denies us the power to redefine the social order according to Gospel values. I have never in my life known a hostess who said to a late-arriving guest, "There is not enough for you," or, "You are not welcome here," yet we priests are encouraged to say it at any Mass where there might be "unworthy people" or "people who do not understand." This is what happens when the "way of the dynamo" takes over and represses the "way of the Virgin," and when *logos* trumps *eros* or ethos. *The corruption of the best is always the worst,* and we end up being neither feminine or masculine, but merely *neutered* and neutral, which means we are unable to be generative and pass on real life.

MATERNAL AND FEMININE IMAGE OF GOD[11]

Francis's ideal of an all-inclusive community—or family—seems to have developed from, or been influenced by, a strongly maternal concept of God. Erich Fromm describes the maternal concept of God in this way:

> In the matriarchal aspect of religion, I love God as an all-embracing mother. I have faith in her love, that no matter whether I am poor and powerless, no matter whether I have sinned, she will love me, she will not prefer any other of her children to me; whatever happens to me, she will rescue me, will save me, will forgive me.[12]

Psychologically speaking, this seems to be the concept of God that Francis enjoyed. It might be a natural result of his closeness to his own mother, Pica, and his possible rejection of the father image as seen in his pained relationship with his own father, Pietro. In my years of teaching in many cultures, I have found Erich Fromm's insight to be continuously true: "The character of the love of God depends on the respective weight that each group gives to the matriarchal and patriarchal aspects of religion."[13]

Performance-based cultures seem to worship a masculine god (or is it the other way around?). Relation-based cultures, or those longing for it (as in Latino Catholicism), almost always prefer a feminine god, and if they don't get it they find it anyway, as we can see in their—for all practical purposes—worship of Mary. The more macho a culture, the more you will see images of Mary. (I remember counting a full eleven prominent images of Mary in a Catholic church in a cowboy part of Texas. Male Jesus was only found hanging on the cross.)

Fromm speaks of matriarchy as more characteristic of humble and unpretentious people. It seems evident that Francis's love for his Father in heaven—and for Jesus—was even a maternal type of love. He transferred this love-character to all those things that he held most dear; at various times he referred to Rome, the Portiuncula, and his beloved "Lady Poverty" as "mother." He even considered himself to be a mother to his friars. Once in a dream he saw a little black hen with innumerable little chicks that could not all get under her wings. He woke and interpreted the dream in this way:

> I am the hen, by nature small and black, and the Lord has given me many children whom I cannot protect by my own strength.[14]

Most of all, however, Francis encouraged his friars to be "mothers to one another" and that "every one of them should love and take care of his brother like a mother loves and takes care of her son."[15] When speaking of religious life in a hermitage he tells the friars:

Let two of them act as the mothers, and have the other two as their children. And *the brothers who are the mothers should guard their children from everything.*[16]

His different attitude is even evident in the very structural setup of the order, where patriarchal and hierarchical titles were forbidden and replaced with the words like "guardian" and "servant," which is often translated in English as "minister." In his first Rule he says, "Let no one ever be called 'prior,' but all in general shall be called lesser brothers."[17] Our recent ministers general now sign their official letters "Brother" and not "Father"; yet Rome will no longer allow "brothers" (non-ordained) to be superiors in our communities, which means Francis could not be a superior in his own order today! And this, after Vatican II told us to return to our unique charisms! When the religious sisters actually did just this, Rome seemed to say, "Well, we did not really mean that."

The maternal character of love seems to permeate Francis's idea of love, and reflects the "courtly love" tradition from the twelfth-century troubadours of France that clearly influenced him. Courtly love highly idealized women, poetry, music, and male *courtesy* (a word he uses frequently) toward all things feminine, weak, or poor. It was in this period that most of the great churches in Europe were built and, almost universally, given female names: Our Lady, Frauenkirche, Notre Dame, St. Mary of something, and La Signora of something. None were named "Christ the King" to my knowledge. The combination of massive masculine constructions and yet very feminine-style liturgies, music, and vestments inside seems to speak of a certain synthesis that is still longing to fully manifest.

It seems that when God is also allowed to be Mother, then all the children line up as equals, their value not based on performance but on having been born from her same womb, just as God loves all of her [sic] creatures equally and unconditionally, "has no favorites" (Acts 10:34), and "makes no distinction between one and another" (15:9).

We know that, in the presence of both a true God and a good mother, each of us feels ourselves to be, in fact, *the favorite*, which is exactly what the Jewish people concluded from Yahweh's maternal way of relating to them. The Jews knew they were uniquely "chosen," protected, and loved "among all the peoples of the earth" (Deuteronomy 7:7ff.), as Francis and Clare so delightfully discovered too. Every mystic comes to the same conclusion, which is precisely what makes each of them a mystic.

CHAPTER NINE

The Legacy of Clare:
Living the Life at Depth

> When the Blessed Father saw that we had no fear of poverty, hard work, trial, shame, or contempt from the world, but instead we held them in great delight, he created a form of life for us.[1]
>
> —RULE OF ST. CLARE

FRANCIS'S RECOGNITION AND HONORING OF the feminine, that was such an important part of his life and teaching, took concrete and personal shape in the person of Clare. She has usually been overshadowed by her partner, Francis, in the public imagination; in her writings, she seems to see herself that way very humbly, as we see in this wonderful opening quote. But Chiara Offreduccio (1193–1253) has finally begun to emerge as her own person, with her own unique identity, writings, and message. She was not just Francis's feminine counterpart, but also had her own strength, message, and identity.[2]

Many cultures have tended to see women largely as appendages to men, as daughters and wives, and almost as property. My mother signed her name "Mrs. Richard Rohr" and thought nothing of it. That sense of ownership of women is evident in the brutal attempts that Clare's twelve male relatives made to recapture her (and later her sister, Agnes) from San Paolo in Bastia after her Palm Sunday departure from their family home when she decided to join Francis. But we can no longer be content, nor would Francis be content, nor will history be content, with such a limited understanding of Clare. We know too much now— about her, her equal and parallel calling, and her beautifully independent spiritual journey. Her subsequent treatment by history is a lesson in how we all suffer when the feminine is overlooked, subsumed, or even denied.

Clare's letters and writings are so consistently upbeat, positive, hopeful, encouraging to others, and lovingly visionary that we can only conclude that she faced her demons down, dove into the negativity that all of us avoid in ourselves and in the world, and came out the other side as clear light or *Chiara*. Clare allowed herself no place to run or hide, and lived for forty years in one little spot of earth, outside the walls of Assisi, called San Damiano. She was both a master and mistress of letting go of all that was unnecessary or unimportant. She went inside instead of outside, and subsequently discovered the outside to be a perfect mirror for the grace she had already found within—and vice versa. Clare went deep instead of far, low instead of high—and thus redefined both high and low. Breaking all records, the formal process for her canonization began only two months after she died.

Many friars often felt that Francis was a bit of a fanatic in regard to poverty, whereas Clare just quietly lived it. After Francis, his Friars Minor moved toward an extroverted, education-oriented lifestyle that made it impossible, or at least highly impractical, to be honestly "poor." Once you are educated into various institutions, you have access and connections and are not really powerless anymore. Francis's radical poverty was soon forgotten, deemed impossible, or quietly rejected, for it placed him in a different social class than men prefer, quite specifically the "minors" and not the "majors."[3] This very real change of social class was glossed over by many of his male followers; they usually understood such downward mobility in an ascetical or private way, but without the clear message for society or the Church that we see in Francis and Clare. The social critique was gone. Franciscan poverty was just too "radical," too strong a judgment on the rest of the Church and on society.[4]

Only Clare and her sisters created a way for the radical life of Francis to be actually lived with freedom and joy. The common name for the sisters, "Poor Clares," emerged in the vernacular of many languages and reveals the social statement they were seen to be making. *Clare absolutely insisted on "the privilege of not being obliged to receive privileges, the right to live without any rights, the guarantee of living without guarantees."*5 How countercultural can you get?!

Though Francis lived and taught a radical humility, the friars in his order moved from their original humble lives into a status- and role-conscious male society, and soon into a clerical domain where humility was neither admired nor sought after. In the male world, humility commonly looks like weakness, lack of exposure to the "real world," or even low self-esteem; but it is not an admirable virtue or any kind of needed strength. Laypeople and women often put clerical men to shame here.

Clare, however, created a humble lifestyle of "structural humility"—where she and the sisters could not fake humility but had to live and love their own ordinariness day by day—living in a closed community with few distractions. There was no place to hide from themselves or from God. There was no one to impress, no one who needed to be impressed by their cloistered life except God alone. I remember that same wonderful freedom in my own enclosed novitiate in 1961, and it was probably why I asked my novice master if I could stay for one more year with "God alone." He said no. I had to grow up and get educated!

CLARE AND THE CONTEMPLATIVE LIFE

In her third letter to Agnes of Prague, Clare wrote: "Place your mind before the mirror of eternity! Place your soul in the brilliance of glory! Place your heart in the figure of the divine substance, and through contemplation, allow your entire being to be transformed into the image of the Godhead itself, so that you may feel what friends feel, and taste the hidden sweetness that God has reserved for His lovers."[6]

This profound quote, that could only emerge as a fruit of contemplation, along with her very frequent use of the mirror metaphor in her writings, communicates to me that Clare experientially understood prayer as an actual transformation of the self, a reflected glory, even daring to speak of "allowing your entire being to be transformed into the image of the Godhead itself."[7] This was surely not common Catholic language in the Western Church at that time and would have seemed presumptuous or even heretical to many (as it may even seem today).

Clare directly expresses what the Eastern Church held onto under the name of divinization (*theosis*). *Theosis* was understood as *a true, objective sharing and growing in our divine nature*, which was then reflected and received in humans as in a mirror. All we can really do is polish our own mirror to reflect the gift of this Godself more perfectly.[8] Thus the objectively given "image" at our conception becomes subjective "likeness" over time, building on the foundational metaphors that we were created in both *the image and the likeness* of God (Genesis 1:26).

Clare also perfectly maintained an important theological balance by saying that it was a true transformation that was taking place, and yet it was also a *mirroring*, a reflection from Another. We humans do not create this reflection by any personal performance. Jesus was seen as the perfect mirror of the Godhead himself, which he then reflected onto us (2 Corinthians 3:18). In one of her rather short letters, she uses the image of mirror eight times.[9] Clare was an orthodox Christian believer, which is to say she was not a pantheist ("all things are God—and I am too"), but a total pan*en*theist ("God is *in* me, I am *in* God, and God is in all things"). That provides an entire life agenda for Clare, as the full Gospel was meant to do. Divine intimacy is more than enough to live on, and makes poverty, celibacy, and obedience no burden. But without such regular mirroring, these values cannot really be lived or loved, but only create bachelors and old maids.

Practiced contemplation was not always the strong suit of the Friars Minor, whereas it was always front and center for the Poor Clares. When such contemplative seeing was regularly rediscovered by the friars, it invariably created a whole new reform movement (called variously Alumbrados, Illuminati, Recollects, Reformati, Observants, and Capuchins). Only now are we recognizing the rather universal loss of the actual "how" of contemplation among both male and female communities after the Counter-Reformation and Enlightenment. After those cultural movements, all of the orders largely "recited" prayers and "attended" formal liturgies rather than being taught how to find inner quiet or emotional freedom from themselves. There are very few experienced teachers of the true contemplative mind even to this day. Most still think of "contemplative" as being introverted and taking some quiet time, but seldom as knowing how to develop an alternative consciousness that is ready for God. The older tradition of contemplation is only being rediscovered in our time, after Thomas Merton and others pulled back the veil and revealed that we had all lost it—for centuries now.[10] It was quite a loss, as I hope you are convinced after reading chapter five.

The older practices of contemplation were *formally* taught by very few Franciscans, like Bonaventure, Francisco de Osuna, and Bernardino de Laredo. Clare herself was not a teacher, but her writings and her ability to remain so positive over such a long period (forty-one years) of enclosure reveal that she had discovered true contemplation. I am sure it was practiced in a de facto way by many of those who followed her and Francis, but the "prayer of quiet" learned by the desert fathers and mothers and retained in Eastern Church monasteries was rather universally lost after the dualistic Christian fighting of the Reformation and the heady rationalism of the sixteenth through the twentieth centuries.

Teresa of Ávila (1515–1582) recognized this loss when she tried to practice what was then called "mental prayer." She called Francisco de Osuna "a bait for her soul" because he introduced her to the older contemplative tradition and taught her what to actually do with the racing mind and obsessive emotions that control almost all of us.[11] Like most of us, she was given a diet of recited prayers, but almost no inner methods or effective practices to deal with inner demons, fixations, fears, emotions, angers, and wounds. Somehow she and John of the Cross found this grace largely on their own, by the clear lead of the Holy Spirit. But they had to found new and separate houses to practice it, and were persecuted by their own!

The common sign that the contemplative mind has been accessed is when you see people who are *highly capable of long periods of silence and solitude—and do not become negative or narcissistic in the process—but actually increase in joy and love.* This is not possible if you have a dualistic mind or still operate from the egoic level. The early friars ran to their caves and wattles to find this clear soul of contemplation, while the women faced down their demons in the safety of enclosures that soon spread all over Europe. Nothing else was possible for women at that time, but it also allowed them to become the "holding tank" that created the necessary depth and stability for the entire Franciscan experiment.

After the sixteenth century, the Poor Clares, like all of us, only learned the older tradition of the prayer of quiet by default and through the Holy Spirit (Romans 8:26). I am sure many learned it through their own intense desire and good will, but it was no longer systematically taught anywhere that I know of. Franciscans by my time were all on our own, and many candidates and novices felt cheated when they never actually "made contact" with a loving God. Many faced early disillusionment at the very possibility of prayer, when their elders only gave them the scaffolding (telling them to "say" the Office, "attend" the Mass), but seldom the substance. "Fighting distractions" is an impossible goal ("Don't think of an elephant"); it sent us on the wrong course toward *willful* concentration instead of the *willing* prayer of receptivity, which the Church had seen in Mary's perfect prayer of "Let it be" (Luke 1:38). The "how" of letting go is so counter to ego consciousness that it has to be directly taught, and can only be taught by people who are already there themselves and know the real obstacles. Almost all thinking is obsessive, but no one taught us that.

The contemplative mind, which is really prayer itself, is not subject to a mere passing on of objective information. *It must be practiced and learned*, just like playing the piano or shooting basketballs. I do suspect that the Poor Clares' overwhelming emphasis on poverty and letting go gave them a head start in understanding prayer as a surrendering more than an accomplishment, an acquisition, or a performance that pleased God. They were already experts in self-emptying (*kenosis*) and letting go. In other words, poverty is first of all for the sake of prayer, and not totally an end in itself.

CHANGED PRIORITIES

For Franciscans, male or female, the first priority was *living the spiritual life in a visible way that shouted Gospel love*! A "form of life" (which is what both Francis and Clare called their Rules) was merely their strategy for getting there. Their life, close to the bottom, was where they hoped to learn the science of love. Their small communities were to be audiovisual aids in living and disseminating the transformative power of the Gospel, which was primarily a school of love. Francis and Clare taught us to put Jesus and his message in front, but also to enjoy and make use of the wisdom and protection of the Church as the only available vehicle for that very message, while also critiquing it as a frequent obstacle. You can see that critique of the hierarchy in some of the sermons of St. Anthony of Padua in the twelfth century and St. Bernardino of Siena in the fifteenth century. Francis and Clare themselves never critiqued the Church with words, but surely by the utterly countercultural nature of their lives.

The Catholic Church gave the friars and sisters foundation, access, and protection, even if it did tend to make us overly codependent on its sole explanations and dispensations. It also—ironically—gave us the scriptural, spiritual, and theological tools by which to critique its own structures and practice, which is the only way to critique anything—from the inside out. This is a great shock and surprise for many of us, and I am convinced that it is why Catholicism tends to produce so many great souls. You have to learn non-dualistic thinking to survive happily inside of any total institution. Catholics are often masters at "yes, and," without even knowing it.

Ordained friars, however, learned that it is very hard to criticize the very vehicle that is giving you your status, your identity, your employment, and your public standing as a "minister." We were and are much less free than the sisters and the "lay" brothers. The Poor Clares were able to enjoy a certain kind of freedom, as have many contemplative communities, by not getting involved in active or sacramental ministry at all. This is, of course, an intentional self-limiting that sometimes has its own kind of problems. Many enclosed communities tend to take on the holiness, the personality, the eccentricity, and even the anger or unique devotional practice of any long-term abbess. That is a big risk. If she is a whole and holy woman, of course, it is a huge blessing and advantage, as it was for Clare's original community.

So just as Clare was overlooked in favor of Francis, Clare's hard-won virtues and spirituality were often overlooked in favor of the male and

Western virtues of achievement, success, and performance. The friars became, for good and for ill, the public face of Franciscanism for most people; literally, in most cases, since Poor Clares until recently often lived behind screens.[12] Most later Franciscan sisters, however, followed a "Third Order" rule and became active in ministry and service, which would probably be the most common "Franciscan" sisters that you would know today. You may have met their smiling faces from Allegany, Oldenburg, Tiffin, Rochester, Milwaukee, Clinton, Philadelphia, La Crosse, Rio Rancho, Wheaton, Reading, and Little Falls—and that is just a few of their motherhouses in America, from which they do a thousand and one ministries that many others are not free to do. Most of their founders had to fight for these ministries and for their unique mission, which usually meant fighting Rome, bishops, and priests, I am afraid.[13]

Without Clare's radically simple gospel lifestyle, grounded in contemplation, male Franciscans often became sloppy in our vocation, largely extroverting what should have been an interior life. This is nobody's fault, no bad will, nothing against men (I am one myself!), but this is just what happens when you have too much outside and not enough inside, too much busyness and not enough groundedness, too many roles and functions instead of contemplative prayer, too much male bravado and performance without much intimate presence and silence.

The sisters, quite simply, kept our feet to the fire of authentic interiority and intimacy with God. We male Franciscans often became complex "human doings" instead of *simple human beings*. Clare was a simple and "clear" human being first. On some levels her biography and writings are spare and seemingly naïve, and that is also her light. Yet I know she had to suffer her way through to such a "second simplicity," as I call it in *Falling Upward*. Such a journey to fullness, after having gone through all of the trials and complexity of early and midlife, is the final fruit of contemplation and integrity. Clare really models for us an utterly grounded "second-half-of-life person," even when she was chronologically in her first half.[14]

A Spirituality for All

Clare protects and offers us a contemplative spirituality for both women and men, for celibates and partnered, for extroverts and introverts (although, I admit, more for introverts), for people with souls and bodies, and even people both Christian and non-Christian. Using our "beyond the birdbath" metaphor, Clare's kind of wisdom helps us take flight in a very different way. Her life was so uncluttered, with such depth and clarity in choosing and facing human limitation, that she created a *lifestyle that made both depth and divine encounter highly possible, emotionally necessary, and normally inevitable.* That would summarize my admiration of her and her chosen lifestyle, and why she ends up grounding the whole Franciscan enterprise in truth and in depth.

Sometimes even popes can be poetic, as we hear in the sermon that Alexander IV preached at her canonization in 1255: "Hidden within, she extended herself abroad. Yes, she hid, yet her life has now come to light. Chiara was silent yet her fame is now proclaimed everywhere. She lived in a small cell, and will henceforth be known in the cities of the world."[15] She is one of only a handful of women whose personal writings have come down to us from the first thirteen hundred years of Christianity, even though she was minimally educated. Hers is the first Rule for women that we know of. That is what inner experience and spiritual education can do for the soul and for us.

Ken Wilber, the contemporary Thomas Aquinas on things philosophical and spiritual, sums up Clare's final experience when he says, "If the doors of perception are cleansed, the entire Cosmos is your lost and found Beloved, the Original Face of primordial Beauty, forever and forever, and endlessly forever. And in the face of that stunning Beauty, you will completely swoon into your own death."[16] And that's exactly what Clare did!

Her final recorded words seem to indicate this very phenomenon, almost as if she is joyfully watching her own departure and trustfully speaks directly to her own soul in beautiful feminine images: "Go forth now, you have a good escort. The one who created you has provided for you. The one who created you will guard you as a mother does her little child."[17]

For Clare, her ending is assured and set in motion by her beginning, as it is, in fact, for all of us (Ephesians 1:4–6). But she knew it, claimed it, and loved it, and thanked God "for letting her live."[18]

Now she herself serves as a trustworthy *escort* for those of us who follow after her.

CHAPTER TEN

Entering the World of Another:
Francis and the Sultan of Egypt

If I tell them, they will consider me a fool; if I am silent, I cannot escape my conscience.[1]

—FRANCIS, BEFORE WARNING THE CHRISTIAN CRUSADERS

THE CONNECTION THAT FRANCIS MAKES with "the enemy" in his lifetime might end up being his most powerful statement to the world about putting together the inner life with the outer, and all of its social, political, and ethnic implications. He also offers an invitation to—and an example for—the kind of interfaith dialogue that provides a much-needed "crossing of borders" so we can understand other peoples at even basic levels. Like few other incidents in his life, Francis's meeting with the Sultan of Egypt took him far beyond the usual saccharine portrayals of him. Francis's kind of border crossing is urgently needed in our own time, when many of the exact same Christian-Muslim issues are at play all over again.

Francis's several attempts to visit the troops fighting in the Holy Land, and his unparalleled visit with the Sultan, Malik al-Kamil, in September 1219 in Damietta, Egypt, have been brought to a much more critical and effective level by the recent scholarly works of several distinguished authors.[2] These three studies, all very accessible, succeed, in my opinion, in bringing this unparalleled historical event out of the shadows of pious hagiography into the realm of very real social, political, and spiritual importance.

The Cultural and Religious Context

It is significant to realize that the mistrust, fear, and hatred between the East and West in the thirteenth century, and between Christianity and Islam, matches if not exceeds what we are facing today. There was almost no actual knowledge of Islamic culture or religion in Europe at that time, even among the educated and the popes, but rather only scary stereotypes of "the enemy."

The vast majority of voices in the Western Church—popes at their lead—had been swept up in the fervor of the anti-Islamist Crusades which began in 1095. There were nine Crusades; Francis intervenes in the fifth. Popes repeatedly used promises of eternal life and offered indulgences and total forgiveness of sin for those who would fight these "holy wars" that were then backed up by kings and official Crusade preachers. Hardly anyone objected or recognized that this was a major abuse of power and of the Gospel itself.[3]

Sometime around the beginning of the Crusades, the until-then recognized sin of "simony" (see Acts 8:9–24, where simony came to mean any payment to receive sacraments, favors, offices, or ordinations) for some reason stopped being a sin. It vanished, just like the sins of usury and violations of Sabbath rest, when it was no longer culturally admired or needed. Conservative Catholics love to think that the Church is *semper eadem,* "always the same." A true knowledge of history shows that is not at all the case, and, in fact, quite the opposite.

Francis knew that the Crusades were justified by no less than St. Bernard of Clairvaux, who had preached the disastrous Second Crusade, and by several popes, and that they were encouraged by a Crusader flag and the oft-quoted motto *Deus Vult* ("God wills it"). He nevertheless said that it was *not* God's will that Christians win the Crusades and that this war "is against the will of the Lord."[4] This was really quite testy and revolutionary for his time. Some scholars believe that even Bonaventure played down this fact in his "official" biography in order to make Francis more attractive to Rome and the Christian "patriots." Until recent scholarship, most Franciscans made little of this supposed event, thinking most of it was a pious legend. I did myself.

WHAT FRANCIS DID

Francis left his own culture at "great cost" to himself to go to the Sultan, to enter the world of another—and one who was considered a public enemy of his world and religion. He seems to have tried three times, but only succeeded in getting fully to his goal on the third try. This third time, he went to Egypt primarily to tell his own Christian troops that they were wrong in what they were doing (that is, in fighting the Fifth Crusade preached by Pope Innocent III and other Catholic leaders). Francis warned that the battle, and the war itself, would fail.

It is notable that he preached to the Christians (not the Muslims) and, "with salutary warnings, forbade the war, and the reasons for it, but truth was turned to ridicule and they hardened their hearts and refused to be guided."[5]

Probably Francis's entire attitude toward enemies, and therefore toward Islam, is best summarized in chapter twenty-two of his first Rule, which some scholars now think was his closing address to the chapter of friars before he left for Egypt, since he thought he would probably never return. He may have thought it would be his final testament to them. It surely sums up his own attitude, which frankly is at a very high level of non-dual consciousness. And, as with Jesus himself, most of us either-or thinkers might just glaze over this quote in disbelief, doubting that anyone could really say it and mean it:

> Love your enemies, do good to those who hate you. Our Lord
> Jesus Christ himself, in whose footsteps we must follow,
> called the man who betrayed him his friend, and gave

himself up of his own accord to his executioners. Therefore, our friends are those who for no reason cause us trouble and suffering, shame or injury, pain or torture, even martyrdom or death. It is these we must love, and love very much, because they give us eternal life.[6]

His humility and respect for the other, and thus for Islam, gained him what seems to have been an extended time, maybe as much as three weeks, with the Sultan. The Sultan sent him away with protection and a gift (a horn that was the Islamic call to prayer, and is still preserved in Assisi), which says that they had given and received mutual regard and respect.

There is no precedent that we know of for this kind of behavior in the medieval period. After Francis, the only other Franciscan I am aware of who made such contact is the Majorcan, Raymond Lull (1236–1315). He made at least seven trips to the Arab world, and sought a neutral vocabulary that all three monotheistic groups could hear, perhaps even discovering the Enneagram tradition for such purposes.[7] He taught that prayerful transformation—not war—would help Muslims and Christians get beyond their mutual belligerence.

With great wisdom, Francis was able to distinguish between institutional evil and the individual who is victimized by it. He still felt compassion for the individual soldiers, although he objected to the war itself. He "deeply grieved" over the impending battle, and "mourned" the soldiers, especially the Spaniards because of what he called their "greater impetuousity."[8] He realized the folly and yet the sincerity of their patriotism, which led them, however, to be *un-patriotic* to the much larger kingdom of God where he placed his first and final loyalty.

Francis made it clear to his friars in his most primitive Rule that the first way of being among "the Saracens" is "not to engage in arguments or disputes, but to be subject to every human creature for God's sake and to [be content] to confess that they [themselves] are Christians." (Today, we call that the "ministry of presence.") We can only assume this is what he himself had done in 1219, and he then urged that friars should only resort to formal *preaching* if they could "see it as God's will," a phrase (*in'shallah*) that he might have learned from Islam's common use of it.[9]

In Francis, as in Jesus, the turnaround of consciousness was complete: the enemy of the small self became the friend of the soul, and he who lost his small life could find his Great Life. Only such a new person can take on the social illnesses of our time, or any time, and not be destroyed by cynicism.

One wonders, however, if the dualistic and contentious mind that we now take as normative can understand, allow, or support this kind of radical spirituality—or any leaders who would talk this way today. My sense is that we have not progressed much beyond the exact dilemma that Francis stated in 1219: "If I tell them they will consider me a fool, but if I am silent, I cannot escape my own conscience."

The only difference is that there are people like you reading this kind of book, and hopefully allowing it to stir your heart, awaken your mind, and give firm step to your feet. This is not just the higher consciousness of Francis of Assisi; it is actually *conscience* itself.

CHAPTER ELEVEN

Bonaventure:
To Yield to Love Is to Return to the Source

Christ has something in common with all creatures. With the stone he shares existence, with the plants he shares life, with the animals he shares sensation, and with the angels he shares intelligence. Thus all things are transformed in Christ since in the fullness of his nature he embraces some part of every creature.[1]

—BONAVENTURE

THERE IS NO OTHER TEACHER who takes the vision of Francis and Clare to the level of a total theology and philosophy, a fully symmetrical worldview, as well as Bonaventure of Bagnoregio (1217–1274). In my view, he was to Francis what Paul was to Jesus. Both are less "radical" in some ways than those they interpret, but both help followers and thinkers to know what Jesus's and Francis's lives might be teaching us in a more systematic way.

They both seem to say, "If this is true, then this is what it implies." Bonaventure's writings are so extensive, broad, brilliant, and poetic that I can only give you a small taste here. Étienne Gilson, the great medievalist, says that the teaching of Bonaventure "marks the culminating point of Christian mysticism and constitutes the completest synthesis it has ever achieved."[2] You are in for a treat.

Bonaventure is called the "Seraphic Doctor" of the Church because his writings are so filled with the warmth and fire that was associated with the Seraphic order of angels. He is probably an exemplary Franciscan mystic because he so effectively pulls his brilliant head down into his fiery heart, and he integrates contemplation with an extremely active life, as we hear in one of his more oft-quoted verses, all the more amazing because he was such an intellectual:

> Seek grace not instruction, desire not understanding,
> Seek the groaning of prayer over diligent reading,
> Seek the Spouse more than the teacher,
> Seek God not man, darkness not clarity,
> Not light but the fire itself.[3]

BONAVENTURE'S VISION OF GOD, LIFE, AND FAITH

For readers who are more familiar with the language of medieval fire and brimstone, worthy and unworthy, sin, guilt, merit and demerit, justification and atonement, that has taken over in the last five centuries, when you read Bonaventure, you will find little or none of that. His vision is positive, mystic, cosmic, intimately relational, and largely concerned with cleaning the lens of our perception and our intention so we can see and enjoy fully!

He starts very simply: *"Unless we are able to view things in terms of how they originate, how they are to return to their end, and how God shines forth in them, we will not be able to understand."*[4] For Bonaventure, the perfection of God and God's creation is quite simply a full circle, and to be perfect the circle must and will complete itself. He knows that Alpha and Omega are finally the same, and the lynchpin holding it all in unity is the "Christ Mystery," or the essential unity of matter and spirit, humanity and divinity. The Christ Mystery is thus the template for all creation, and even more precisely the crucified Christ, who reveals *the necessary cycle of loss and renewal* that keeps all things moving toward ever further life. Now we know that the death and birth of every star and every atom is this same pattern of loss and renewal, yet this pattern is invariably hidden or denied, and therefore must be revealed by God—which is "the cross."

Bonaventure's theology is never about trying to placate a distant or angry God, earn forgiveness, or find some abstract theory of justification. He is all cosmic optimism and hope! Once it lost this kind of mysticism, Christianity became preoccupied with fear, unworthiness, and guilt much more than being included in—and delighting in—an all-pervasive plan that is already in place. As Paul's school says, "Before the world was made, God chose us, chose us in Christ" (Ephesians 1:4). The problem is solved from the beginning. He could have helped us move beyond the negative notion of history being a "fall from grace" and invited us into a positive notion of history as a slow but real emergence/ evolution into ever-greater consciousness of who we are.

In Bonaventure's world, the frame of reality was still big, hopeful, and positive. One reason he was able to do that, as we can see in many Catholic mystics, is that he was profoundly Trinitarian, where the love always and forever flows in one positive and forward direction. That was both his starting point and his ending point. Most of Christian history has not been Trinitarian except in name, I am sad to report; it has largely been a worship of Jesus who was extracted from the Trinity— and thus Jesus apart from the eternal Christ (see chapter fourteen), who then became more a harsh judge of humanity than a shining exemplar of humanity "holding all things in unity" (Colossians 1:17–20).

Bonaventure's strong foundation in the Trinity gave him a non-dual mind to deal with the ineffable mystery of God and creation. A dualistic mind closes down at any notion of Trinity, because it cannot process it. God, for him, is not an offended monarch on a throne throwing down thunderbolts, but a "fountain fullness" that flows, overflows, and fills all things in one exclusively positive direction. Reality is thus in process, participatory; it is love itself, and not a mere Platonic world, an abstract idea, or a static impersonal principle. God as Trinitarian Flow is the blueprint and pattern for all relationships and thus all of creation, which we now know from contemporary science is exactly the case.[5]

I am personally attracted to Bonaventure because of his strong sense of cosmic wholeness, what some called "the Great Chain of Being" and maybe today we would call ecosystems, or the circle of life. I am also drawn to his strong sense of paradox, which theologian Ewert Cousins finds to be key to the understanding of his writings and which he rather cleverly names "the coincidence of opposites."[6] After reading Bonaventure, the crossed lines of the crucifix henceforth become a geometric metaphor for all the seeming contradictions in the world—which, if held with compassion, create deep wisdom in the soul. It thus rightly became our symbol for redemption itself,[7] and it is no surprise that the cross became our central "logo," our own Christian "sign of Jonah" (Luke 11:29).

The right angles of the cross can be seen as the eventual "cross purposes" of almost all of reality—and there Jesus hangs, and from there he teaches. Bonaventure was clearly a non-dual thinker who could see in wholes; even his teaching on contemplation is a thirteenth-century crash course on what we now have rediscovered and call "centering prayer." It is well summed up in the seventh chapter of his *Journey of the Mind to God*. Bonaventure was practiced in and taught the older understanding of contemplation that was largely lost after the various dualistic fights of the sixteenth through twentieth centuries. You will not find these formulations of the older contemplative prayer of quiet until Francisco de Osuna, Teresa of Ávila, and John of the Cross again discover it in the sixteenth century, and which Thomas Merton then rediscovers in the twentieth century.

Bonaventure's Theology

Bonaventure's "vision logic," as Ken Wilber would call it, and the lovely symmetry of his theology, can be summarized in what he himself named as the three great truths that hold everything together for him:

Emanation (we come forth from God bearing the divine image; our very DNA is found in God).

Exemplarism (everything, the entire chain of being, and everything in creation is an example and illustration of the one God mystery in space and time, by reason of its "origin, magnitude, multitude, beauty, plenitude, activity, and order"[8]).

Consummation (we return to the Source from which we came; the Omega is the same as the Alpha and this is God's supreme and final victory).

What a positive and safe world this describes! In Bonaventure's teachings we have a coherent and grounded meaning that the postmodern world no longer enjoys—and yet longs for. Note that this is clearly *not* the later reward/punishment frame that almost totally took over when people did not *experience* God, but only believed propositions. Most people today are not sure where we came from, who we are, and where we are going, and many do not even seem to care about the questions.

What if we could recover a view of the world and God that was infused with Bonaventure's teaching? It would provide a foundation that we lack in our often aimless and adrift age. Do you think it is possible for us to regain such a positive worldview again? It could be the "cosmic egg" that could hold our lives together during times of despair and cynicism. Our later limited notion of individual salvation works much better if it is all held together inside of a primary cosmic salvation; the part then replicates the whole. Right now, it feels like we are all on our own. There is no *whole* to be a part of!

Bonaventure described the Great Chain of Being both in a historical and linear way—but also in terms of cosmic connectedness *along* the way! He was following Paul in Colossians: "In his body lives the fullness of divinity, and in him you will find your own fulfillment" (2:9–10), or "There is only Christ: He is everything and he is in everything" (3:11).

We were created in unity, proceed forward insofar as we are in unity, and return to God's full gift of final unity, according to Bonaventure's reading of the Gospels. It is grace before, during, and after.

For Bonaventure creation is quite simply the mirror and image of God, and he uses metaphors like footprint, fingerprint, effigy, likeness (*vestigia Dei*) to make his point in different contexts. This unitive vision is very similar to that of the later Jesuit Teilhard de Chardin (1881–1955). These two teachers first gave me the confidence to believe and teach that "everything belongs." They both describe and defend the universal belonging of all creation, and show us that such a cosmic divine victory makes the fear-based preoccupations of later exclusionary and punitive Christianity seem so small and unnecessary.

I regret to say that there has been a massive loss of hope in Western history, a hope still so grandly evident in Bonaventure. (Are not the World Wars of Christian countries a clear sign of this loss? Genocides are surely a symptom of deep self-loathing and fear.) His God was so much bigger and more glorious than someone to be afraid of, or the one who punished bad guys—because his cosmos was itself huge, benevolent, and coherent. Did his big God beget an equally big and generous cosmos? Or did his big cosmos imply a very big God? You can start on either side. For many in our time, an initial reverence for the universe leads them to then reverence whoever created this infinity of Mystery and Beauty. As Francis said while looking at the stars one night, "If these are the creatures, what must the creator be like?" I see this same humble awe in many great scientists today. Cosmology is the new name for much theology now.

The entire universe is about connection and relationship—from the smallest atom to the galaxies and everything in between. Sin and evil emerge when we try to stand outside of that circle of connection. Bonaventure's worldview was not only coherent but also dynamic. He believed that if you name and honor things correctly, everything then takes care of itself. Most of mainline Christianity never stated identity clearly and proudly; humans were invariably presented with a tentative identity. ("You *might* be a daughter of God, if you are a *good enough girl*—and that only *in the future*." "This might be God's world, but it is mostly the kingdom of Satan.") Such wagering and guessing leaves us all adrift and afraid, and is not a solid foundation for faith or love.[9] True Gospel, as Bonaventure saw it, gives you both identity and hope *now*.

ON BONAVENTURE'S LEGACY

Bonaventure was indeed a great philosopher and a theologian, but first he was always a passionate believer, a Christian, and, of course, a friar. He was a grand exemplar himself of action and contemplation as a tireless worker and traveler for the friars for over seventeen years, when he probably would have much rather stayed in Paris as a teacher. Yet these are the very years when he wrote his greatest and most profound books. If he had stayed in academia, many say his full systematic teaching would have complemented and rivaled that of Thomas Aquinas, who was there at that same time. But Providence allowed him to learn, teach, and write as a worker in the fields instead of a professor at a university. Maybe that changed everything, and even kept him quintessentially Franciscan.

Bonaventure's practical, problem-solving side, however, was perhaps also his dark side. He is partly responsible for the "clericalization" of the Friars Minor, and for the diminished role of the so-called "lay brother" (even though Francis was likely a lay brother himself, as were most of the first generation). But the humble services of brothers did not pay the bills, whereas educated clerics brought in stipends and status for the struggling and quickly growing order.[10] He was trying to help his fledgling group gain stability and credibility, which was part of his job as minister general of the order. Form and fashion so often follow function, and he wanted to make his ragtag group "fashionable" and orthodox.

Bonaventure also made his biography of Francis the official one, and, in the process, repressed other versions in various ways. His desire was to prevent the soft piety and legend that was developing around Francis at that time and has continued to this day. But Bonaventure's censorship has denied us many important early sources. He even glossed over some of Francis's peacemaking efforts with the Muslims to make his order more acceptable and orthodox in the view of Rome (which had fully encouraged the Crusades).[11] He similarly hedged his bets with the radical poverty of Francis, which he knew would not be sustained or justified in the eyes of popes and bishops—or the friars themselves.

Probably, for Bonaventure, the Jungian aphorism holds true: "The greater light you have, the greater shadow you cast." Maybe just saying this will allow us to be patient with our own and each other's (and Bonaventure's) shadow side too. Even saints have their blind spots. Our own role and place in a group often determines what we can see and what we cannot see—or say. This is why we have as one of our core principles at the Center for Action and Contemplation, "Practical truth is more likely found at the edges and at the bottom of most groups." That is why Francis always wanted to stay close to the "bottom" and at the edge; it is the only way to be prophetic. I would call Bonaventure a mystic, a theologian, and a brilliant teacher, but not a prophet as Francis was. (I would say the same of Paul in relationship to Jesus.) He paid a price for being at the head of his order and in academia for so many years. There is a legend that he was washing dishes when they brought him the cardinal's hat, and he told them to hang it on a tree. I hope and trust the story is true. He clearly was a very humble man.

Finally, I would offer Bonaventure as an exemplar of how one's own mystical experience can and must be trusted, and how it can still be made accountable to both Scripture and tradition. Bonaventure quotes the Bible generously, and loves to build on creative biblical metaphors. He surely knew the Great Tradition, from the Hebrew Scriptures to Augustine to Dionysius to Richard of St. Victor to Peter Lombard. He then combined these traditional sources in a most lovely and coherent way. Bonaventure thus appeals to our sense of reasonableness and order without being tied to the later and limited idea of "rational." This is a balance very hard to achieve for those of us who have come after the Enlightenment.

It is important to know that *the opposite of faith is not doubt, but in fact, certitude and the demand for certitude!* Bonaventure lived beautifully on the cusp of a broad and deep combination of knowing—along with not knowing, "un-speaking," and silence. He loved Reality itself first and then garnered fruitful metaphors to point us toward a love affair with that very Reality. Bonaventure *invites and inspires with a poetic clarity more than he declares or defines with any demanding certitude.* They are two very different styles.

Bonaventure is surely and totally Christian, and yet he presented universal truth and themes in such a way that a mystic from any religion would and could appreciate his teaching. His Christ is bigger than any single Christian denomination can hold, which has been appreciated down to Protestant theologians in our own time.[12] He is an early Teilhard de Chardin and even a "process theologian" seven centuries ahead of time,[13] although, of course, Teilhard had the advantages of modern science, telescopes, and cosmology that Bonaventure could only dream about. I also cannot hesitate to say that if Bonaventure overheard the present and futile debate between creationism *or* evolution, he would humbly say, "I don't see the problem." He would recognize that *God has brilliantly created things that continue to create themselves*, and God is so humble, patient and hidden out of sight that he or she lets us (or science) take all the credit. God is quite willing to be an *anonymous donor* to his creation, and remains fully hidden except to those who desire to see. "Above the heavens and in the mouths of babes God has perfected praise" (Psalm 8:1–2), Jesus quotes to all those filled with denial or resentment (Matthew 21:16). But there is neither denial nor resentment in Bonaventure. His heart was never stingy, but always generous and eager to love.

Bonaventure's "tree of life," his "coincidence of opposites," his "journey of the soul to God," his Great Chain of Being, each made joyful room for everything in one divine circle of life. God for him is "a circle whose center is everywhere and whose circumference is nowhere." And now you know that all things, you included, live safely and happily inside of that one good circle.[14]

CHAPTER TWELVE

John Duns Scotus:
Anything but a Dunce

Knowledge is the product of both the knower and the thing known.[1]

—John Duns Scotus

The unkind word "dunce" is a pejorative of the little town of Duns in southern Scotland where John the Scot was born and raised. His thinking was so subtle, brilliant, and hard to understand that his opponents later mocked him by calling his professor's hat at Oxford the "dunce's" cap, meaning the cap of someone who is incapable of learning. Just a little trivia to get you intrigued with one who is indeed very intriguing.

Scotus was a philosopher theologian who joined the early group of Franciscans who had first came ashore at Canterbury in 1224 while Francis was still alive. We know little about his biography, but the fact that he would join this new ragtag group with no academic credentials tells you a lot about his priorities. His tomb in Cologne, Germany, in the Minoritenkirche where he died in 1308 at the age of forty-two, says in Latin, "Scotland bore me, England taught me, and Germany holds me."

Although for many he is an unknown figure, we Franciscans tended to study his philosophy over that of Thomas Aquinas, and I was blessed to have four years to distill his rarefied wisdom at Duns Scotus College in Michigan in the early 1960s. Some of Scotus's seminal ideas have come to their fullness and deep appreciation in our own time, but these three especially stand out:

1. The "univocity of being" which gives a philosophical foundation to what we now call the circle of life or ecosystems, holons and fractals (parts that replicate the whole), unitive thinking—and mysticism itself.

2. His assertion that inside of such wholeness God only creates particular individuals, a quality he named "thisness" (*haecceity*), which has endeared him to poets and mystics alike, and utterly exemplifies and grounds the principle of incarnation in the concrete and the specific. To Scotus, even Mary was believed to be a *particular and unique choice* of God, and he is credited with laying the philosophical-theological foundation for what became the official doctrine of the Immaculate Conception, which had not been the mainline position up to that time. For Scotus, Mary personified and accentuated "thisness," or "the

scandal" of God's particularity. Even fervent Catholics often hesitated to think that God would make just one exception to the universal pattern of brokenness ("original sin").

3. His assertion that Divine Incarnation itself was "the first idea in the mind of God" and not an after-the-fact attempt to solve the problem of sin. Scotus, in effect, taught that grace is inherent to the universe from the moment of the "Big Bang" (implied in Genesis 1:2, which has the Spirit hovering over chaos). His cosmic Christology implies that grace is not a later add-on-now-and-then-for-a-few phenomenon, but the very shape of the universe from the start. The Christ Mystery (Inspirited Matter) is Plan A for God—and not a Plan B mop-up exercise after "Adam and Eve ate the apple."

These are three world-changing ideas. *One changes your philosophy, the second your cosmology, and the last your foundational Christian theology.* First, let me offer a short thought on the univocity of being, because it is a foundational concept, especially for mysticism: Our being is not just *analogous* to God's being, but we may speak of our two supposedly different beings "with one voice." From this alone we know that Scotus was a non-dual thinker, and thus a contemplative.

The Univocity of Being

I am convinced that Scotus was laying the philosophical foundation for what Michael Talbot and Ken Wilber in our time are speaking of as a *holographic* universe, where "everything is a holon,"[2] and also Mandelbrot's discovery of fractals, the repetitive and imitative patterns found in nature, mathematics, and art. In these discoveries, we know that the part contains the whole or replicates the whole, and yet each part still has a wholeness within itself—this "appreciative accumulation" is what makes the whole Whole! We now believe such wholeness is true physically, biologically, and spiritually, and can even be seen as a basis for any understanding of mystical union. It implies that there is an "inherent sympathy" between God and all created things, and between the other "ten thousand things," too. Each of us replicates the Whole and yet has a certain wholeness within ourselves—but we are never entirely whole apart from connection with the larger Whole. Holons create a very fine language for what I call *the mystery of participation*, for understanding how holiness transmits and how God's life is an utterly shared phenomenon. If you are "holy" alone, you are not holy.

Salvation is not a divine transaction that takes place because you are morally perfect, but much more it is an organic unfolding, a becoming who you already are, *an inborn sympathy with and capacity for*, the very One who created you. Each is both a part that is like the Whole and also contributes to the Whole, just as Paul teaches in his analogy of the body (1 Corinthians 12:12–30). The world we live in today no longer enjoys any natural sense of this wholeness, and therefore of holiness.

In our secular mind, we do not inherently and naturally "participate" in this creation, but we think we have to "buy" our way in somehow. This tragic spiritual loss takes many forms today. It is a sad and lonely world as a result, and we live outside the gates of paradise—excluded by angels of our own making (Genesis 3:24).

In this chapter, however, we will primarily be discussing the other two great themes of Scotus since the univocity of being has been implied in the whole book thus far. I surely cannot teach these other two ideas in the fully academic and footnoted way they deserve; that is the work of much more qualified scholars.[3] But I can follow the Franciscan call and strategy to bring great truths and scholarship to the common person and the ordinary Christian, so everyone can profit and grow from them. Just as bad theology has been used for purposes of slavery and oppression, good theology—made available in simple form to the masses—offers much needed liberation to both individuals and society. That is my hope and vocation.

"THISNESS"

So why is "thisness" (Scotus's doctrine of *haecceity*) so good and important? To begin with, such thinking was a breakthrough in the hierarchical Middle Ages, when the top and the center were alone considered important. If the top held, people assumed they could hold on too! Any writing about a common person or an ordinary person's life was very, very rare at that time. The concept of the individual apart from the group had not yet been born, despite Jesus's talk of leaving the ninety-nine to search for the one. Kings and queens, the papacy, the office of the bishop, and nationhood were far more important than anything local, immediate, concrete, or any specific "this." "My king is better than your king" and "my religion is the only true one" substituted for most personal transformation or any sense that God was engaged with the individual and ordinary soul (which is precisely mysticism). The corporate, the ninety-nine, the ethnic identity were preferred to the individual soul, which is exactly why most wars could be waged at all. This is "first-tier" or tribal consciousness.

For John Duns Scotus to move beyond tribal consciousness to honor the specificity of the individual—while still fully balancing this with the social Body of Christ—is really quite amazing. Such a leap is only possible if there has been a death to the ego, and the beginnings of communal wisdom.[4] We are, in fact, still moving toward this synthesis that Scotus exemplified: the common good *and* the individual good are equally important—and must be held in a hard-won but creative tension. Few achieve it, in my opinion.

Scotus mirrors Jesus leaving the ninety-nine sheep and going after the one. But, just like Jesus, he holds that "one" fully inside a "commonwealth" (the word works here!), so *he is no Western individualist.* That would be to cheapen his insight. He is fully an incarnationalist, which is our great Christian trump card. The universal incarnation always shows itself in the specific, the concrete, the particular, and it refuses to be a mere abstraction. No one says this better than Christian Wiman: "If nature abhors a vacuum, Christ abhors a vagueness. If God is love, Christ is love for this one person, this one place, this one time-bound and time ravaged self."[5]

The doctrine of *haecceity* is saying that we come to universal meaning deeply and rightly through the concrete, the specific, and the ordinary, and not the other way around, which is the great danger of all the *ideologies* (overarching and universal explanations) that have plagued our world in the last century. Everything in the universe is a holon and a fractal—and thus important! The principle here is "go deep in any one place and you will meet all places."

When we start with big universal ideas, at the level of concepts and -isms, we too often stay there—and argue about theory, forever making more distinctions. At that level, the mind is totally in charge. It is then easy to "love humanity, but not any individual people." We defend principles of justice but would not put ourselves out to live fully just lives ourselves. Only those who live like Francis and Clare do that. This takes different forms on the Left and on the Right, to put it in political terms. Liberals love political correctness itself and get authoritarian about process and language as recently defined. Conservatives love *their validating group* for its own sake and become authoritarian about its symbols, forever defining and defending the rules and rights of membership in that group. Both sides risk becoming "word police" and "symbol protectors" instead of actually changing the world—or themselves—by offering the healing energy of love.

Sometimes neither group ever gets to concrete acts of charity, mercy, liberation, or service. We just argue about its theory and proper definition. I have done it myself. Making our thinking first of all particular, now, concrete, and individual is a major gift from Scotus, and his entire philosophy makes love, and *the will to love in a particular way*, more important than intellect or understanding, or any theories about love itself.

In fact, this is often quoted as the essential difference between Scotus and Thomas Aquinas. For the Franciscan School, before God is the divine Logos ("rational pattern"), God is Eternal Outpouring ("Love"). The *divine pattern is first and itself Love,* as opposed to thinking that God can be rationally understood, and that this God then orders us to love. Love is then a mandate instead of the nature of being itself. For Scotus, as for Bonaventure, the Trinity is the absolute beginning point—and ending point too. *Outpouring Love is the inherent shape of the universe*, and when we love, only then do we fully *exist* in this universe.

We do not need to "understand" what is happening, or who God is, before we can live in love. The will to love precedes any need to fully understand what we are doing, the Franciscan School would say.

This is a major difference in schools of spirituality, and I must say that the post-Reformation Church lived almost entirely inside of the Thomistic school instead of the Franciscan: understanding was a higher goal than "the will to love." Almost all seminaries taught Thomas Aquinas first, and even exclusively, except for some Franciscan seminaries. Many papal decrees over the centuries made Thomism almost tantamount to the Gospel itself. I am sure you can see how it kept us a few shades away from a more mystical and unitive reading of the Gospels. In short, *truth was equated with knowing instead of loving.* Josef Pieper, a Thomist scholar himself, rightly said that "The proper habitat for truth is human relationships."[6] Ideas by themselves are never fully "true," which is Platonism and not incarnate Christianity. At that level, we just keep arguing about words, and this keeps us from love.

ATONEMENT THEORY

For the sake of simplicity and brevity here, let me say that the common Christian reading of the Bible is that Jesus "died for our sins"—either to pay a debt to the devil (common in the first millennium) or to pay a debt to God the Father (proposed by Anselm of Canterbury [1033–1109] and has often been called "the most unfortunately successful piece of theology ever written"). Scotus agreed with neither of these readings. He was not guided by the Temple language of debt, atonement, blood sacrifice, or necessary satisfaction, but by the cosmic hymns of Colossians and Ephesians (see chapter fourteen).

If Scotus's understanding of the "how" and meaning of redemption (his "atonement theory") had been taught, we would have had a much more positive understanding of Jesus, and even more of God the Father. Christian people have paid a huge price for what theologians after Anselm called "substitutionary atonement theory": the idea that, before God could love his creation, God needed and demanded Jesus to be a blood sacrifice to atone for a sin-drenched humanity.

Please think about the impossible, shackled, and even petty God that such a theory implies and presents.[7] Christ is not *the first idea in the mind of God*, as Scotus taught, but a mere problem solver after the sad fact of our radical unworthiness. And where did that come from? When you start with a negative, it is almost impossible to ever get back to anything positive and wonderful. When you start with a positive, things tend to take care of themselves from within.

We have had enough trouble helping people to love, trust, and like God to begin with, without creating even further obstacles. Except for striking fear in the hearts of those we sought to convert, substitutionary atonement theories did not help our evangelization of the world. It made Christianity seem mercantile and mythological to many sincere people. The Eternal God was presented as driving a very hard bargain, as though he were just like many people we don't like. As if God could need payment, and even a very violent transaction, to be able to love and forgive his own children—a message that those with an angry, distant, absent, or abusive father were already far too programmed to believe (this common and highly operative assumption needs deep healing in many people, and was at the heart of my early men's work).[8]

Scotus, however, insisted on the absolute and perfect freedom of God to love and forgive as God chooses, which is the core meaning of grace. Such a God could not be bound by some supposedly offended justice. For Scotus, the incarnation of God and the redemption of the world could not be a mere reaction to human sinfulness, but in fact *the exact, free, and proactive work of God from the very beginning.* We were "chosen in Christ before the world was made," as Paul says in Ephesians (1:4). Sin or problems could not be the motive for divine incarnation, but only perfect love! The Christ Mystery was the very blueprint of reality from the very start (John 1:1). *God's first "idea" was to pour out divine infinite love into finite, visible forms.* The Big Bang is our scientific name for that first idea, "Christ" is our theological name, and it is all about love exploding itself out in all directions. For Scotus, God never merely reacts but always *supremely and freely acts*, and acts totally out of love.

It is no wonder that Christianity did not produce more mystics and saints over the centuries. Unconsciously, and often consciously, many people did not trust or even like this Father God, much less want to be in union with him. He had to be paid in blood to love us and to care for his own creation, which seems rather petty and punitive, and we ended up with both an incoherent message and universe. Paul told us that "love takes no offense" (1 Corinthians 13:5), but apparently God was the big exception to this rule. Jesus tells us to love unconditionally, but God apparently does not. This just will not work for the soul or mature spirituality.

Basically when you lose the understanding of *God's perfect and absolute freedom and eagerness to love*, which Scotus insisted on, humanity is relegated to the world of *counting*! Everything has to be measured, accounted for, doled out, earned, and paid back. That is the effect on the psyche of any notion of heroic sacrifice or necessary atonement.[9] It is also why Jesus said Temple religion had to go, including all of its attempts at the "buying and selling" of divine favor (John 2:13–22). In that scenario, God has to be placated and defused; and reparation has to be paid to a moody, angry, and very distant deity. This is no longer the message Jesus came to bring.

This wrongheaded worldview has tragically influenced much of our entire spirituality for the last millennium, and is still implied in most of the Catholic Eucharistic prayers. It gave lay Catholics and most clergy an impossible and utterly false notion of grace, mercy, love, and forgiveness—which are, in fact, at the heart of our message. The best short summary I can give of how Scotus tried to change the equation is this: *Jesus did not come to change the mind of God about humanity (it did not need changing)! Jesus came to change the mind of humanity about God.* Christ was Plan A for Scotus, the hologram of the whole, the Alpha— and therefore also the Omega—Point of cosmic history. Understand the beginning and you know where it is all heading. This was, of course, very similar to Bonaventure's notion of emanation and consummation.

God in Jesus was trying to move people beyond the counting and measuring that the ego prefers to the utterly new world that Jesus offered, where God's abundance has made any economy of merit, sacrifice, reparation, or atonement both unhelpful and unnecessary. Jesus undid "once and for all" (Hebrews 7:27; 9:12; 10:10) all notions of human and animal sacrifice, and replaced them with his new economy of grace, which is at the heart of the gospel revolution. Jesus was meant to be a game changer for the human psyche and for religion itself.

In other words, we are all saved by grace and the utter freedom of God to love who and what God wills, without our tit-for-tat thinking getting in the way of God's absolute freedom, and absolute freedom to love. As Peter already says to the first apostles when the Holy Spirit descends on the unbaptized and they want to deny this very possibility: "God has no favorites" (Acts 10:34–35). Ironically, when we experience God's love we feel very much like a favorite!

We all need to know that *God does not love us because we are that good; God loves us because God is good.* Nothing humans can do will inhibit, direct, decrease, or increase God's eagerness to love. That is the one Absolute of biblical faith, as Pope Francis says, and all else is relative to it. All other claims to some theoretical "absolute truth," even by the Church, are all in the head, and that is not where we need truth. For us, the word has become flesh. So we need to first find truth in relationships and in ourselves, and not in theories. Only great love can handle great truth.

Such good teaching on so many foundational issues should make us very happy indeed. For me, the Jesuit poet Gerard Manley Hopkins crystallized so beautifully the effect that Scotus's teaching has on mystical minds:

Yet ah! this air I gather and release
He lived on;
These weeds and waters, these walls are what
He haunted
Who of all men most sways my spirits to peace.[10]

The worldview of John Duns Scotus can and still will sway our spirits to this same cosmic peace: God is good and so we his children must be good too; God is free and so we do not need to be afraid of true freedom; God is nonviolent love, and this is the only hope for a world in which even Christians think violence is a way to "redeem" the world. Wrong ideas about God create wrong ideas about everything else too.

CHAPTER THIRTEEN

Francis: A Natural Spiritual Genius

I did not know what love was until I encountered one that
kept opening, and opening, and opening.[1]

—CHRISTIAN WIMAN

IF YOUR ONLY GOAL IS *to love, there is no such thing as failure.* Francis
succeeded in living in this single-hearted way and thus turned all failure
on its head, and even made failure into success. This intense eagerness
to love made his whole life an astonishing victory for the human and
divine spirit, and showed how they can work so beautifully together.

That eagerness to love is the core and foundation of his spiritual genius.
He encountered a love that just kept opening to him, and then passed
on the same by "opening and opening and opening" to the increas-
ingly larger world around him. He willingly fell into the "bright abyss,"
as poet and faith writer Christian Wiman calls it, where all weighing
and counting are unnecessary and even burdensome. After his conversion, he lived the rest of his life in an entirely different economy—the

nonsensical economy of grace, where two plus two equals a hundred and deficits are somehow an advantage.

Such transformation of the soul, both in the inflowing and in the outflowing, is the experiential heart of the Gospel for Francis of Assisi. He then brought the mystery of the cross to its universal application (far beyond the Christian logo), for he learned that both the receiving of love, and the letting go of it for others, are always a very real dying to our present state. Whenever we choose to love, we will—and must— die to *who we were before we loved*. So we often hold back. Our former self is taken from us by the object of our love. We only realize this is what has happened after the letting go, or we would probably always be afraid to love.

No wonder that God signed the stigmata, "the brand marks of Jesus" (Galatians 6:17), on Francis's body at the end of his life. I think this means that Francis learned the message, price, and glory of love in the very cells of his body. Full knowing is always psychosomatic knowing, and Francis seems to exemplify someone who fully absorbed the Gospel with his entire being, not just with his head. Some call this "kinesthetic knowing," and I would also call it kinesthetic believing.

The "Life Flow" of Francis

"Marrow of the Gospel" is the phrase Francis used to describe his Rule of 1221,[2] which scholars now agree is surely his essential and radical message, even though it was never formally approved by Rome. Here it is clear that he wanted his followers to know the Gospel as a "form of life" and a flow of life, and not just as juridical commandments or doctrinal statements. As you might expect, in Rome's eyes, this rule was a mere stitching together of Scripture quotes—which they undoubtedly presumed the friars already knew and were living. But without accusing anyone, Francis clearly paid attention to very different texts than organized Catholicism had emphasized. Thus his first Rule seemed naïve and harmless to them, and so he had to clarify it and make it more juridical. Francis asked for the help of Brother Bonizo, who was a canon lawyer, to create something more to the point, measurable, and thus enforceable. That became the Roman-approved Rule of 1223, which we have to this day, and which is still quite simple and radical.

But, in time, Francis emerged as an utterly compelling image more than any rule or doctrine, a practical lifestyle more than any new institution, nature itself more than the Church apart, a startling happiness more than a theological explanation, and a poem more than any prose, which forces us to ask: Who really is this man? Centuries later, we still join Brother Masseo, who said to him: "Why after you? Why after you? Why does the whole world come running after you, Francis of Assisi?"[3] And they still do.

Perhaps the greatest Protestant theologian of the twentieth century, Paul Tillich, praised Francis's revolutionary life in many ways, and even called him "the father of the Renaissance" because he succeeded in overcoming the accepted split between religion and the natural world. Tillich felt that Francis "in the long run undermined Catholic supernaturalism" because he showed that everything was supernatural for those who knew how to see.[4]

Yet, in our time, there are those who do not see his importance. The very conservative commentator George Weigel, in his book on the Catholic theology of war and peace,[5] seems to feel that Francis is a marginal character, not to be taken seriously, who Weigel says is "outside the mainstream of Catholicism." He is unfortunately right in saying that Francis might be outside the mainstream of Catholicism, but terribly wrong in feeling that he is not to be taken seriously. Francis will always be a threat to any who wish to preserve and idealize a nostalgic past, a separate superiority, or any self-serving status quo.

A Living Answer

I surely do not have a full answer to the question of why Francis continues to be so attractive, but let me say a few things, since I promised to talk more about the source now that you have seen some of the flow. Francis does not really provide many systematic answers to theological questions as much as he *is* a living answer to those who are asking the right questions. Mother Teresa served the same function in the twentieth century. We look to them for what they did—how they lived the heart of the Gospel—rather than for theology or doctrine. Neither of them is usually quoted in academic papers. Pope Francis is also a living answer before he is asked any questions. The cardinal electors must have wondered what they had just done as soon as he opened his mouth.

My personal belief is that mainline, organized Christianity has too often missed out on the freedom and joy of the Gospel and often settled for something nice, proper, and culturally accommodated. It was organized into a formal religion that did indeed become a living spirituality for many people. But the common variety of church life in most denominations could be called "fast-food" religion instead of deeply nutritious meals that feed and change people at deep, unconscious levels. Verifiable statistics of attendance, donations, service, and involvement make that overwhelmingly clear. Christianity has largely reflected current cultural values, and even bourgeois values, during most of its history. Alfred North Whitehead, however, put it somewhat unkindly: "Modern religion has tended to degenerate into a decent formula whereby people can embellish an otherwise comfortable life."[6] I wish that were not true.

I am not saying that those who "embellish an otherwise comfortable life" are infidels, lost, unloving, rejected by God, or any less than I am. But there is strong evidence now that much of our history in all denominations has proceeded from the "first tier" of human consciousness, where the concerns are largely security, order through power, and belonging.[7] There were always exceptions, but there is not much evidence that the common denominator of clergy or laity ever rose much above first-tier consciousness, even down to our own time. Most church life, and even much religious life, has been a belonging system that gave good people a workable self-image, which is a necessary place to start in the first half of one's life.[8] But it is not close to the radical and risky, and often dark, *search for God and faith* that characterizes Francis and so many saints and mystics.

Two recent popes have said that a lot of clergy are "careerists" (their word) who have found an admired occupation for themselves, instead of being people on the costly search for God or seeking to actually serve others. I sadly find that often true. We tend to conduct or *attend services* instead of actually *serving* "pro bono," or just *for the good of it*, which is often left to humble volunteers and lay associates. We friars were originally meant to be non-stipendiary ministers of the Gospel, which is the core meaning of mendicancy. I remember how surprised I was, immediately after ordination, when people insisted on giving me money for what I just thought I was supposed to do, and was eager to do, for free! It was my job and a privilege. Sorry to say, I eventually adjusted.

For Francis, the medium had to be the same as the message, the training the same as the ministry—or the message itself would get quickly lost. Only love can search for, give, or receive love. It is almost that simple. Our problem, however, is often at the structural level much more than it is a harsh judgment about any individual. Francis created a very different classroom for his followers, sort of an "underground seminary" if you will, where you had to live faith before you talked about faith. Our Rule was initially just "tips for the road," an itinerant and mendicant lifestyle, both an urban plunge and total solitude in nature *where love could be tasted and touched*, much more than a formal seminary classroom where it might just be defined. But, as we have mentioned before, movements that do not institutionalize do not tend to last, so we had to do just that for the sake of stability and continuity. Yet Francis had positively challenged things at their foundation, rather than just rearranging them on the surface, and, in so doing, often exposed the common root problem. In that sense, he is rightly called "a radical" (*radix* = root) and a prophet.

DRAWING US FORWARD

Francis was a living exemplar of where we are all being attracted and led. Just as the Cosmic Christ serves as the Omega Point (Teilhard de

Chardin) for all of history, Francis is also a prime attractor forward, or what the Scholastics called a "final cause" (see chapter sixteen). They both draw humanity forward just by walking the full journey themselves. Transformed people quite simply transform people, and set the bar of history higher for all of us. That is how we fundamentally "help" other people, much more than the codependent forms of helping.

If we ourselves are totally at the first tier of consciousness (security and order needs), or even the second (need for answers and explanations), and if the structural expectations are also at those levels, we have almost no ability to even minimally understand the what, why, and who of a third-tier person like Francis, or like Jesus himself, who all agree represents the highest level of non-dual consciousness ("I and the Father are one," John 10:30). Yet both of them have largely been interpreted by cultures and churches still living at the first tier of consciousness. Do you see the problem? We all tend to dumb down such profound humanizers and divinizers to our own comfortable level and actually have little curiosity or ability to care about their major message.

The developmental experts say that the best humans can do, and that on a very good day, is perhaps understand someone a bit beyond ourselves. Being invited forward by prophets and mystics, yet invariably offering great resistance, is the clear pattern of history. We sadly know this to be true in recent centuries from the lives of Abraham Lincoln, Gandhi, Nelson Mandela, Dorothy Day, many UN secretaries general, and Martin Luther King, Jr. We do not usually love more advanced people, but quite often hate and fear them. Francis is really an amazing exception. He somehow succeeds in being loved, admired, and imitated by even non-Christian religions and very secular people to this day.

So God gives us highly evolved people to pull us all forward. The Christian word for that was simply "saint." We cannot imagine something until we see it as a living model or archetypal figure. Then it constellates in our consciousness as maybe possible for us too. Through his story, Francis is still greasing the wheels of consciousness and holiness. It then rubs off and spreads out by osmosis. I felt this strongly when I was invited recently to accompany the Dalai Lama. He said little beyond "My religion is kindness," but the stadium was packed, and the lines reached across the Ohio River bridge in Louisville just to see him or perhaps touch him. Many pointed out the direct line between that event and Thomas Merton's presence down the Kentucky road at Gethsemani Abbey. Merton, Mother Teresa, Pope Francis, and the Dalai Lama are all good examples of Prime Attractors in our own time.

In the true meaning of the word, Francis's energy was contagious, or, as the Gospels put it, "power went out from him" (Luke 8:46). The

Eastern religions have tended to understand the importance of a living model more than we have, and ashrams and disciples soon gather around them. We canonize saints only after they die, almost as if we do not know how to recognize the real thing while they are here. In many countries where I have taught, people watched my eyes, my smile (or lack of it), my gestures, my neediness, my peace (or lack of it), and that became the primary message that affected them or disaffected them— much more than my theologizing and my sermons. If my expressions and energy were off, my teaching was largely a waste of their time.

The Divine Trickster

God gave Francis to history in a pivotal period when Western civilization began to move into pure mind, into functionality, into consumerism as sufficient for human meaning, and also into a world of perpetual war. He was himself a soldier and his father was a tradesman in cloth. He came from the very world he was then able to critique, but he offered a positive critique of these very systems at the beginning of their now-eight centuries of world dominance. As Adolf Holl put it, he emerged precisely when we started "putting clocks into church towers."[9] When we started counting, Francis stopped counting. He moved from the common economy of merit to the scary and wondrous economy of grace, where God does not do any counting, but only gives.

Exactly when we began to centralize and organize everything at high levels of control and fashion, Francis, like a divine trickster, said, "Who cares!" Right when Roman Catholicism under Pope Innocent III reached the absolute height of papal and worldly power, he said in effect, "There is another way that is much better!" Exactly when we began a style of production and consumption that would eventually ravage planet earth, he decided to love the earth and live simply and barefoot upon it. Francis of Assisi is a Prime Attractor to what we really want, what we definitely need, and who we finally are. And apparently he did it all with a "perfect joy," which finally makes all of the difference!

People are only afraid of death as long as they do not know who they are, but once you know that you are objectively a child of God, you are already home and your inheritance is given to you ahead of time. Then you can begin living and enjoying instead of climbing, proving, or defending. Your false self, all religions say in one way or another, must "die before you die." Only then can we sincerely say with Francis, "Welcome, Sister Death"! I have faced the first death, and I lost nothing that was real. And so, "the second death can do me no harm," as Francis says in his "Canticle of the Creatures." Death itself will only "keep opening, and opening, and opening," and I think that is exactly what we mean by resurrection.[10]

All of this creates a very different form and shape to our spiritual life. It is no longer elitist or separatist or competitive, but changes our deepest imagination in the direction of ever greater simplicity. This imaginal world will not normally change until we place ourselves, or *are placed*, in new and different lifestyle situations. As we say in one of our core principles at the Center for Action and Contemplation, "You do not think yourself into a new way of living, you live yourself into a new way of thinking." Francis and Clare displaced themselves into different worlds where their hearts could imagine very different things and they had to pay attention to something other than comfort or convenience.

THE TRANSMISSION OF ENERGY

Poet and essayist Christian Wiman has said, "To walk through the fog of God toward the clarity of Christ is difficult because of how unlovely, how 'ungodly' that clarity turns out to be."[11] I sadly agree with this quote because there is a shock involved when we suddenly see that incarnation is actually our ordinary life, now, everywhere. At first, it is a disappointment. But once we become practiced at a contemplative worldview, a "thisness" way of seeing, there is nothing trivial anymore and all is grace. But those who have chosen a split world of sacred *or* profane don't know how to live in a world where everything is sacred. Everything is almost too clear, and yet too "ungodly," in that very clarity.

Each thing in creation just *does itself,* as the poet Gerard Manley Hopkins says, and in the very doing of itself as self, it reveals and pulls us into the Eternal Christ. There is henceforth no sacred and secular because the Cosmic Christ has "inscaped" everything with grace from the very beginning. I use Hopkins's created term *inscape* to communicate his honoring of *the ordinary incarnation that everything is,* and his seeing that each thing was "counter, original, spare, and strange," as he learned from John Duns Scotus (see chapter thirteen). Grace is inherent to reality and never just an add-on.

Incarnation must take embodied, singular forms, what Walter Brueggemann calls "the scandal of the particular." It is revealed in exceptional cases, like the stigmata, or the Catholic belief that the Christ could actually be contained in ordinary bread and wine, or in the epiphany that a sexual encounter can contain. Incarnation is always so godly and so ungodly all at once! That is the split that a Christian must overcome, until it is all godly!

The celibacy of Francis and Clare, for example, was certainly a chosen loneliness, as is mine. But it was also a fruitful and positive energy for others in their time, and now for us. It was a choice for "all love" instead of just "one love," which is the choice we are all eventually led toward. Christian Wiman says that "there is an insistence on loneliness that is truly diabolical...but when loneliness passes through love, it assumes an expansiveness and active capacity, and the body becomes an easy channel for the invisible."[12] He, a happily married man, calls this "holy porousness." I know myself that there is also a good meaning to loneliness, which is the chosen celibacy of Francis and Clare. Such people manifest such a pure eagerness to love that they actually incarnate erotic energy in other ways than physical sexuality.

But there is a bad loneliness, too, a negative energy that is based in fear of intimacy or a desire to be special and apart. It is crucial to know the difference, because these two kinds of aloneness offer the world two very different energies: one gives off calm, compassion, and invitation; the other sucks you into its smallness and neediness, or worse, pushes you away. The one is a porous and living cell, while the other is cancerous and sterile. We all need to meet and know—and become— people *whose loneliness has passed through love*, and not just formal celibates or legally married folks. Those who are free in this way do not need you too much, nor do you feel manipulated in their presence. When they give, it is all freedom with no strings attached. *Love is not love until you stop expecting something back. The moment you want something in return for your giving, all love is weakened and prostituted.* This is the nature of the divine energy that transforms; it is inherently contagious, and it is holiness itself. This is Francis and Clare.

Such contemplative minds and hearts are alone prepared to hand on the Great Mystery from age to age, and from person to person. The utilitarian and calculating mind[13] distorts the message at its core. The contemplative, non-dual mind inherently creates a great "communion of saints," which is so obviously scattered, hidden, and amorphous that no one can say, "Here it is," or, "There it is," but instead it is always "among you" (Luke 17:21)—invisible and uninteresting to most, but obvious and ecstatic to the few who seek (Matthew 22:14).

From the Trinity to Jesus, the energetic movement begins, then from Jesus to many like Francis and Clare, to Bonaventure and Scotus, to Hopkins, Teilhard de Chardin, Mother Teresa, Thomas Merton, Dorothy Day, and Pope Francis, and now we ourselves are part of this one great parade, "partners in God's triumphal procession," as Paul calls it, "spreading the knowledge of God like a sweet smell everywhere" (2 Corinthians 2:14), much more a transmission of authentic life than of mere ideas or doctrines.

It is remarkable to know that recent findings about mirror neurons almost *prove* that this energetic movement is the case, even physiologically and interpersonally, and not just pious poetry.[14] If you have never received a gaze of love, you do not even have *the neural ability* to hand it on. You do not know how to do it or what love is. You cannot really imagine love, much less pass it on, until you have *accepted that someone could fully accept you* as you are—and therefore even God could accept you. Before that moment, you will glance downward when the gaze of love or admiration comes your way. I have done it myself, too often.

Human history is one giant wave of unearned grace, and you are now another wave crashing onto the sands of time, edged forward by the many waves behind you. You are fully adopted sons and daughters in God's one eternal family. To accept such an objective truth is the only sense in which you need to be a Christian or a Franciscan. It is the best and deepest understanding of how the Risen Christ spreads his forgiving heart through history. It is not role or office or group that we are passing on—that is not the meaning of "apostolic succession"—it is Love that we are passing on from age to age, and even the very love of God.

Francis has beautifully passed this baton on to those who would receive it. He would not be honored or even interested in us pulling him out of his single place in this eternal Divine Flow and making an exception or idol of him. He himself joined the "great cloud of witnesses" (Hebrews 12:1) and is most honored by *you* now getting in line with everybody else, just as he did in his time. We are saved by simply remaining in the one circle of life and love, and not by standing separate or superior. *This is the One Love that will lead and carry you across when you die.* If you are already at home with Love here, you will quite readily move into the eternal home of Love, which most of us call heaven. Death is not a changing of worlds as most imagine, as much as *the walls of this world infinitely expanding*. If you get love here, you have found the eternal home base, and you will easily and naturally live forever.

Life is never about being correct, but only and always about being connected. *Just stay connected!* At all costs stay connected. Our only holiness is by participation and surrender to the Body of Love, and not by any private performance. This is the joining of hands from generation to generation that can still change the world—and will. *Because Love is One, and this Love is either shared and passed on or it is not the Great Love at all.* The One Love is always *eager*, and, in fact, such eagerness is precisely the giveaway that we are dealing with something divine and eternal.

Lenin is supposed to have said, shortly before he died, "If I would have just had ten Francises of Assisi, my revolution could have worked!" He might have been right. Francis's revolution is still in process and it cannot fail, because it is nothing more or less than the certain unfolding of Love itself, which, as Paul says, "never fails" (1 Corinthians 13:8).

A Dynamic Unity between Jesus of Nazareth and the Cosmic Christ

I am making the whole of creation new.... It will come true.... It is already done! I am the Alpha and the Omega, the Beginning and the End.

—Revelation 21:5–6

I begin with this Scripture passage at the very end of the Bible to ask you a question: Is this Jesus of Nazareth speaking here or Someone Else? Whoever is talking here is offering an entire and optimistic arc to all of history, and is not just the humble Galilean carpenter. This is much more than a mere "religious" message; it is also a historical and cosmic one. It declares a definite trajectory where there is a coherence between the beginning and the ending of all things. It offers humanity hope and vision. History now appears to have a direction and a purpose, and is not just a series of isolated events!

This is the Cosmic Christ who is speaking here. Jesus of Nazareth did not talk this way. It was Christ who "rose from the dead," and even that is no leap of faith once you realize that *the Christ never died— or can die*—because he is the eternal mystery of matter and Spirit as one. Jesus willingly died—and Christ arose—yes, still Jesus, but now including and revealing everything else in its full purpose and glory (read Colossians 1:15–20, so you know this is not just my idea).

When these verses were written, it was sixty to seventy years since Jesus's human body "ascended into heaven." The Christians have now met a fully available *presence* that defines, liberates and sets a goal and direction for life. Largely following Paul, who wrote in the A.D. 50s, they have come to call this seemingly new and available presence a mystery that they address as "both Lord and Christ" (Acts 2:36) more than just "Jesus" (as yet another case of non-duality). They have excitedly come to a sense of Presence that has become more obvious in the world after the Resurrection of Jesus.[1]

Such divine presence had always been there, as we know from the experiences of "Abraham, Isaac, and Jacob" (Luke 20:37–38). But after Jesus, this eternal presence had *a precise, concrete and personal referent*. Perhaps vague belief and spiritual intuition became specific—with a "face" that they could "see, hear, and touch" (1 John 1:1) in Jesus. (In Appendix II, I will try to describe the importance and the power of such a "personal" sense of God.)

THE CENTRALITY OF THE COSMIC CHRIST TO A FRANCISCAN WORLDVIEW

I introduce this theme in a book on Franciscan mysticism because this is the foundational example of how Bonaventure and Scotus took Francis's intuitive worldview and made it explicit and scriptural, and gave it clear theological grounding. They offered the world the eternal Christ as Paul had done, and not Jesus without Christ which has been the norm. This is an important recognition if we want to move beyond mere sentimental and individualistic Christianity. I believe that Francis was unique and ahead of his time for loving and relating to both the historical Jesus and the eternal Christ at the same time, *surely without fully realizing that was what he was doing.* Francis himself just "knew" it and lived it in the way that we described spiritual knowing in chapter five, which is the way most of us intuitively live. Good theology just comes along later and assures us that we are not crazy, and that our deepest intuitions might be touching on something real and true. How else could the Holy Spirit teach us (1 John 2:21)?

Most Christians were never encouraged to combine the personal with the cosmic, or Jesus with Christ; nor were we told that we could honor and love both of them. Nor were we told that it is the same love but just in different frames. To love Jesus makes you an initial believer; to love Jesus Christ makes you into a cosmic believer. Some Eastern

Fathers and early mystics, like Maximus the Confessor, Symeon the New Theologian, and Gregory of Nyssa, brilliantly taught these ideas, but they remained largely undeveloped in the West after the Great Schism of 1054. This is one outstanding example of how the Christ Mystery was portioned out each time the Body of Christ divided (1 Corinthians 1:12–13).

It is important to place ourselves in the largest possible frame, or we always revert back to a very non-catholic ("unwhole") place where both the Savior and the saved ones end up being far too small because Jesus of Nazareth has been separated from the Eternal Christ. Here Christianity becomes just another competing world religion, and salvation is far too privatized, because the social and historical message has been lost. The full Gospel is so much bigger and more inclusive than that: Jesus is the historical figure and Christ is the cosmic figure— and together they carry both the individual and history forward. Up to now, we have not been carrying history too well, because "there stood among us one we did not recognize" (John 1:26), "one who comes after me, because he also existed before me" (John 1:30), to quote John the Baptist.

We made Christ into Jesus's last name instead of realizing it was the description of his cosmic role in history and in all world religions. I fully believe that *there has never been a single soul that was not possessed by the Christ, even in the ages before the Incarnation.* And I believe both well-studied Scripture and the Great Tradition will lead you to the same conclusion. Christ is eternal; Jesus is born in time. Jesus without Christ invariably becomes a time-bound and culturally bound religion that excludes much of humanity from Christ's embrace. On the other end, Christ without Jesus would easily become an abstract metaphysics or a mere ideology without personal engagement. Love always needs a direct object. We need them both and thus we rightly believe in both, *Jesus* and *Christ*, just as most Christians would verbally say.

What We Lost

Paul tried unceasingly to demonstrate "that Jesus was the Christ" (Acts 9:22), just as Peter's affirmation of the same is the first climax of Mark's Gospel (8:29). This synthesis is the heart of Paul's conversion experience, and why he did not think he was abandoning his Jewish faith, but only finding its universal dimension in this "Mystery of Christ" as he loved to call it.[2] Remember, Paul never knew Jesus in the flesh, and hardly ever quotes him directly. He introduced his cosmic understanding with his mystic phrase "*en Cristo,*" and, in fact, uses it more than any single phrase in all of his letters. These seem to be his code words for the gracious participatory experience he so urgently wants to share with the world, and it leads him far beyond either exclusionary Judaism or exclusionary Christianity.

Only in our time is a truly dynamic unity between human and divine, personified and cosmic, Jesus and Christ, being slowly recognized. Up to now, this was an alternative and frankly rare orthodoxy. With our much larger awareness of the universe now, it is timely and even necessary if Christianity is to have any social or historical meaning. After the Council of Nicea (325), we said that Jesus was "consubstantial" with God, and, after the Council of Chalcedon (451), we agreed to a philosophical definition about Jesus's humanity and divinity being united in him; but that non-duality largely remained academic theory because we did not draw out any practical and wonderful implications about history, human evolution, and even ourselves. It remained a static dogma to be "believed," but the evolutionary dynamism it actually introduced was not understood or enjoyed. The results for practical spirituality were minor, I am sad to say, and the results for Christianity and history have been lethal.[3] We lost much of our core transformational message.

"As in him, so also in us, and also in the whole universe" was meant to be our whopping conclusion! What most religion treats as separate (matter and Spirit, humanity and divinity) has never been separate from its beginnings: Spirit is forever captured in matter, and matter is the place where Spirit shows itself. It is one sacred world. As Scotus taught, "Christ was the first idea in the mind of God," and then Teilhard de Chardin

filled out the cosmic schema by calling Christ the very "Omega Point" in all of history! We were supposed to live safely between this Alpha and Omega, with all history moving forward with clear meaning and direction. Without it, we have paddled desperately, and often angrily, in many different directions.

We were not told to understand Christ as the Archetype and Model for all of creation, as Scripture clearly taught (Ephesians 1:3–14; Colossians 1:15–20); but instead we spent most of our time trying to prove that Jesus was "God," which would put our religion out in front of the others and solidify our own ranks. Most Christians, having extracted Jesus from the Trinity, had no overarching schema or explanation for where this God was "coming from" and where their God was leading them, which is precisely back to God. We did not let both Jesus and Christ "hold all things together" as the author of Colossians (1:17) promised. As a result, God had a hard time holding us together too. We became a "text" outside of any meaningful "context." *Jesus always becomes too small if the Christ is forgotten, ignored, or not loudly proclaimed.*

We then found ourselves in a basically incoherent universe that had no center, no direction, and no purpose beyond survival itself (which took the religious form of "saving our souls"). No wonder that science took over as "the major explainer" of meaning. Jesus was indeed a deep and life-changing encounter for a few, but he had almost no historical implications for society itself. Even any initial understandings of "social justice" only began to emerge in the last century! We brought Jesus to the New World, but hardly ever Christ, as we see from our treatment of the natives and the earth (most slave owners were, in fact, "Christians").

The great notion of Christian *salvation* had become a private evacuation plan into the next world for *some very few* humans. God's people did not seem to care much about any "new earth" or the "universal restoration" that the Bible had offered us (Revelation 21:1–2; Romans 8:21–22; *apokatastasis* Acts 3:21). Creation as such did not have much inherent value or purpose, but was merely the backdrop and stage setting for our human-soul-saving, plus the sole resource for our human food and energy. Such "small believing" allowed us to live in this world in a quite narcissistic way. The world remained in that sense very "unsaved" by the Christ who, in fact, came to name it, love it, and free it, "Until God will be all in all" (1 Corinthians 15:28).

Sadly, we now live in a postmodern and largely post-Christian world, which denies any "big story line" or ultimate meaning for history. It is a major crisis and loss of any deep or eternal significance for human civilization, and existentially is experienced as a loss of hope. All the extravagances, technologies, and entertainments will never be able to fill such a foundational hole in the human psyche. In other words, most of the world, and even most of the Christian world, has yet to hear the Gospel!

Few now have the vision to perceive any coherence between the Source and the Goal; only poets and mystics, and some scientists, even bother to think about it. There are always a few, like T.S. Eliot, who says in his "Four Quartets": "In my beginning is my end" ("East Coker," I), and "The end and the beginning were always there...and all is always now" ("Burnt Norton," IV). He saw time itself as redeemed and redemptive. Ironically, we experience such a redemption of time by falling into "an eternal now" (as noted in the work of Jean-Pierre de Caussade, Paul Tillich, and Eckhart Tolle) which pulls together past and future into a wonderful epiphany. We live for such moments when time as mere duration (*chronos*) becomes time "come to a fullness" (*kairos*). At the end of our lives, people do not remember years, months, or days, but only moments, I am told. "The point of intersection of the timeless with time is the occupation for the saint," Eliot says ("The Dry Salvages," V).

In such unredeemed time, the Christian message had less and less significance for thinking people, for scientists, writers, cosmologists, social workers, and those trying to find a purpose and goal for this universe. Check out the dismal European statistics of affiliation with Christianity today, which was the one continent we totally controlled for many centuries. Can a civilization flourish when it hates its own religion? It appears to be of no interest to most Westerners today, not even worth leaving, fighting, or joining. We became merely another moralistic religion (which loved to win over others) which was overwhelmingly aligned with a very limited period of history (empire building) and small piece of the planet (Europe), not the whole of civilization, other races, or any glorious destiny (Romans 8:18ff.). Cosmology itself, however, is becoming the very shape of Christian theology today, as the statistics and range of the universe, and thus the full nature of incarnation, become living data for many of us.

Not surprisingly, therefore, many Christians ended up tragically fighting evolution along with most early human-rights struggles (woman's suffrage, voting rights for those on the margins, racism, classism, homophobia, earth care, justice itself, even slavery)[4], because we had no evolutionary notion of Christ who was forever "groaning in one great act of giving birth" (Romans 8:22). We should have been on the front line of all of these issues, and our bold proclamation of love and justice could have pulled humanity grandly forward. The Christian religion was made-to-order to grease the wheels of human consciousness toward love, nonviolence, justice, and the universality of its inherent message. Mature religion serves as a conveyor belt for the evolution of human consciousness. Immature religion actually stalls us at very low levels of well-disguised egocentricity, by fooling us into thinking we are more moral, holy, or eveolved than we really are.

If it is true, then it has to be true everywhere and all the time. Christianity was uniquely equipped to see this wholeness, and is surely why we first called ourselves "catholic" (*kata holon*, "according to the whole").[5] Yet we had a hard time loving the various parts of creation, so we were ill prepared to love the whole. *Up to now we have been much more into exclusion than inclusion, which is what happens when Jesus is not also Christ.* "Why do you parcel up Christ?" Paul angrily said to the Corinthians (1 Corinthians 1:13).

When we defined Jesus in such a small way, largely as a mere problem solver for sin, we soon became preoccupied with sin itself. In fact, not much was happening in this world except sin and its effects, which clearly became the preoccupation of most monks and almost all of the Reformers. It was a rather small scenario for life, mostly concerned with shame and guilt, atonement and reparation, as if we were merely the frightened children of an abusive father. Maybe that itself was our deepest "sin"? How do you ever get into the great parade when this is the starting line—and "correcting" is God's major concern? Is there no greater meaning to life and history, and Divinity itself? The starting point surely cannot itself be an insurmountable cliff and the goal cannot be only for a very few, or God is hardly God at all. "There is only Christ: He is everything and he is in everything!" (Colossians 3:11), shouts Paul. How could we miss that?

Yes, we formally believed that Jesus was both human and divine at the same time "somehow," but with our largely dualistic thinking, we ended up being *only* human—and Jesus for all practical purposes ended up being *only* divine. We missed the major point—*which was to put the two together in him—and then dare to discover the same in ourselves!* We made our inclusive Savior, that we could imitate and participate with, into a Redeemer that we were told to worship as a quite exclusionary God. Jesus, who was always and overwhelmingly inclusive in his lifetime, seemed to create a religion that had an entirely different philosophy.

We were not assured that we could follow him as "partners in his great triumphal procession" (2 Corinthians 2:14). Instead we were told to be grateful spectators of what he did, and we often missed the redemptive transformation that was offered to us too: "In your minds you must be the same as Christ Jesus" (Philippians 2:5). The Eastern Church called this process *theosis* or divinization, and it is their greatest contribution to worldwide Christianity.[6] But even they did not draw out its very real implications for individuals, much less for society, the poor, or for justice. Totalitarian communism was the sad result in far too many Orthodox countries.

THE IMPORTANCE OF JESUS AS CHRIST

Please do not think me a heretic, but it is formally incorrect to say "Jesus is God," as most Christians glibly do. *Jesus is a third something, which is the union of "very God" with "very man."* For Christians, the Trinity is God, and Jesus came forth to take us back with him into this eternal embrace, which is where we first came from (John 14:3), and this is what it means to have an eternal soul. This is a quite different description of salvation—and, dare we say, the whole point!

This dynamic unity is what makes Jesus the Exemplar, the "pledge" and "guarantee," the "Pioneer and Perfector of our faith" (Hebrews 12:2). Then there is much less *need* to "prove" that Jesus is God (which of itself asks nothing of us); our deep need is to experience the same unitive mystery in ourselves and in all of creation—*"through him, with him, and in him"* as we say in the Great Amen of the Eucharist! This is how Jesus "saves" us and what salvation finally means. The good news is that *we also* are part of the eternal divine dance, but now as the ongoing Body of Christ extended in space and time.[7]

Since we could not overcome the split within ourselves, how could we then possibly overcome it for the rest of creation? The polluted earth, extinct species, tortured animals, nonstop wars, and a deforested planet are the result. It is not so hard to believe in a "second coming of Christ" as it is to believe that he will have anything much to return to on this planet. Yet Jesus the Christ has still planted within creation a cosmic hope, and you cannot help but see it in so many unexplainable and wonderful events and people. The "problem of good" is just as much an enigma and mystery as is the oft-bemoaned "problem of evil."

There were clear statements in the New Testament about a cosmic meaning to Christ (Colossians 1, Ephesians 1, John 1, 1 John 1, and Hebrews 1:1–4; note all are in the first chapters!), and the schools of Paul and John were initially overwhelmed by this message. In the early Christian era, only some few Eastern Fathers (such as Origen of Alexandria and Maximus the Confessor) cared to notice that the Christ was clearly something older, larger, and different than Jesus himself: They mystically saw that *Jesus is the union of human and divine in space and time, and the Christ is the eternal union of matter and Spirit from the beginning of time.* But the later centuries tended to lose this mystical element in favor of fast-food Christianity, almost always dualistic, for the normal parish believer.

The early Franciscan School surely fell in love with the person of Jesus, but then it also saw him as *a corporate personality (a type, an archetype, a model) representing and thus directing the Whole.* We know this by the way that they saw the Christ Mystery mirrored in every aspect of creation, from elements, to weather, to planets, to animals, to attitudes, to non-Christians, to art, and to enemies. Roger Bacon (1214–1292), an early English friar at Oxford, is called "the father of experimental science" because suddenly the natural world was no longer just "natural" for those who had absorbed the Gospel through Francis. *Science was not secular* anymore, although many Christians have still not caught up with this early recognition.

They all built on Francis, who could not see a little lamb without weeping for the Lamb of God or a worm underfoot without thinking of the crucified (Psalm 22:6), because all creation was a mirror of the divine for them. It is one sacramental universe for any who learn how to see fully, as Francis's "Canticle of the Creatures" so beautifully reveals.

THE COSMIC CHRIST AND MYSTICISM

A cosmic notion of Christ takes mysticism beyond the mere individual and private level that has been seen as its weakness up to now. That perception is one of the major reasons that many people mistrust and even dislike "mysticism," because it feels all too private, pious, and mystified, and never gets to the transpersonal, social, and collective levels. False mysticism, and we have had a lot of it, often feels too much like "my little Jesus and my little me," and never seems to make many social, historical, corporate, or justice connections. As Pope Francis says, it is all "too self-referential." If authentic God experience first makes you overcome the primary split between yourself and the divine, then it should also overcome the split between yourself and the rest of creation (thus making the first and second commandments one truth).

For some few, the split is seemingly overcome in the person of Jesus; but for more and more people, *union with the divine is first experienced through the Christ: in nature, in moments of pure love, silence, inner or outer music, with animals, a sense of awe, or some kind of "Brother Sun and Sister*

Moon" experience. Why? Because creation itself is the first incarnation of Christ, the primary and foundational "Bible" that revealed the path to God. The eternal Christ Mystery started about 14.6 billion years ago in an event many now call "The Big Bang" (we are the first generation that can give the first incarnation an approximate number). But God was already overflowing into visible Reality and revealing the God-self in trilobites in North America, giant flightless birds in New Zealand, jellyfish in the oceans, pterodactyls in Asia, and thousands of species that humans have never once seen. But God did. And that was already more than enough meaning and glory.

Surely Neanderthals and "Barbarians," Mayans and Babylonians were not just throwaways or dress rehearsals for an All-Loving God? Did the Divinity need to wait for Roman Catholics and American Evangelicals to appear before the divine show could start? I don't think so. A God known for such universal evidence and fruitfulness could not be that inefficient, unloving, "unvictorious," or unconscious. Creation exists first of all for its own sake, to simply give glory to God. Psalm 104 is a supreme and sustained teaching of this message, and Psalm 98:8 puts it in lovely metaphor: "All you rivers clap your hands, all you mountains shout out for joy at the presence of Yahweh." Sometimes elements seem to know who they are more than humans do. I love to say at Mass, "It is easier for God to convince bread and wine who it is, than to convince us!"

If you have any doubt about what I am saying, this is what I am saying: pre-Christian and even pre-Jewish people already had access to God! This is the *ecclesia ab Abel* ("the church that existed since Abel") that has been spoken of so often in the Fathers and in the documents of Vatican II.[8] From the first righteous victim (Genesis 4:10; Matthew 23:35) until now—*all human suffering cries out to God and elicits divine compassion and human community.* This is a momentous and universal truth. We are indeed "saved" inside the Christ Mystery, and since the beginning of consciousness, which only eventually takes the organized form of "church."

A full Christian, an authentic Franciscan, loves both Jesus and Christ. They can lead with either Jesus *or* Christ, but they eventually must love both. Too many Christians have started and stopped with Jesus, and never known the Body of Christ; and many non-Christians have started with the Christ (under whatever name) and not even known this is what Christians are, in fact, talking about. I have met Hindus who totally live in this hidden Christ, and I have met many Roman Catholics and Protestants who are running away from Christ, as either practical materialists or pious spiritualists. Tertullian (160–225), who is called "the father of Western theology," rightly taught that "the flesh is the hinge of salvation" (*Caro Salutis Cardo*). The incarnation of flesh *and* Spirit is always Christianity's great trump card, yet it often prefers either flesh *or* spirit instead.

If it is authentic mystical experience, it connects us and just keeps connecting at ever-newer levels, breadths, and depths, "until God can be all in all" (1 Corinthians 15:28). Or as Paul also says, earlier in the same letter, "The world, life and death, the present and the future are all your servants, for you belong to Christ and Christ belongs to God" (1 Corinthians 3:22–23). Full salvation is finally universal belonging and universal connecting. Our word for that was "heaven." When any religion scatters instead of gathers it is, in fact, anti-religion.

In the great basilica in Assisi where Francis is buried there is a wonderful bronze sculpture where he is inviting the Holy Spirit, but instead of looking upward as in most paintings, he is looking reverently and longingly downward—into the earth. Francis understood that the Holy Spirit had in fact *descended*, and her location for humans is forever and first of all *here!*

THE "ROCK BOTTOM" MYSTERY

For Christians, the *anointing* ("Christening") of all matter with the Divine Spirit began with Creation itself, as Genesis 1:2 suggests. This anointed nature to physical things is quietly asserted when Jacob "sets up as a monument and anoints" a small rock which he has just used as a pillow, and there he saw a great ladder "with angels ascending and descending" between heaven and earth (Genesis 28:10–18). Before a mere rock, he scandalously says, "How awe-inspiring is this place. It is nothing less than the House of God and the gate of heaven!" For later Judaism and pious Protestants, this surely must have seemed like a mere Canaanite worship of standing stones. Yet Jacob rightly intuits it as a promise and foretaste of the very mystery of incarnation. Jacob, I believe, was seeing and honoring the hidden Christ Mystery and localizing it in a mere rock, which he even calls *Beth-El*, the very house of God.

Later Paul, speaking of the water from the rock that sustained the Israelites in the desert, will say, "They all drank from the spiritual rock that followed them wherever they went. And that rock was Christ" (1 Corinthians 10:4). The Gospel will go further and say that the one who can see Jesus as "the Christ" himself becomes a rock (Matthew 16:18). These are all what I call Post-it Notes that tie together themes from the great unconscious and are nothing we can prove "logically." Yet from Jacob, to Moses, to Jesus, to Peter we have the gradual recognition of the "rock-bottom" mystery: Both the physical world and the human person are revealed as both the hiding place and the revelation place of God; and then, even better for us, we become rocks when we discover this omnipresent Christ Mystery.

I used to preach on contemplative retreats, "Start with a stone!" If you can learn to love and honor concrete, rudimentary, and specific things, it can only build from there. How you do anything is very likely how you do "Christ," and how you do everything. Christians start with Jesus and should end up shouting with Paul, "There is only Christ, he is everything and he is in everything" (Colossians 3:11).

To briefly sum up, I quote the Irish novelist Elizabeth Bowen who says, "*To turn from everything to one face is to find oneself face to face with everything.*"[9]

Jesus is the one face, we are the interface, and Christ is the everything.

APPENDIX II

Is God a Person?
The Franciscan View of the Nature of the Divine

Say not, "I have found the one true path of the Spirit!"
Say rather, "I have wonderfully met the Spirit walking on my
    path."
For the Spirit walks upon all paths.[1]

                        —KAHLIL GIBRAN, *THE PROPHET*

I CONSIDER THE QUESTION OF whether God is a "person" an important
one for any serious understanding of mysticism and the experience of
individual holy people. Yes, most Hindu, Sufi, Jewish, and Christian
mystics, including Francis and Clare, speak—in part—as if God is
quite personal, friendly, and sitting in a chair next to them (a human
writ large), which itself reveals the deep transformative character of
mystical encounters. But we must not conclude that they do not know
what they *are saying* and what they are *not* saying when they speak
of God this way. Lest we dismiss them as lost in a naïve past that we
cannot discover, I am eager to offer the ideas in this appendix.

For many modern and postmodern thinkers, the idea of God, and even more the idea of a "personal God," is passé, an anthropomorphic projection, and thus infantile. Much as these thinkers might admire Francis and Clare, they find their understanding of God too "face to face." They sometimes call it mere "deity mysticism" (as opposed to "formless mysticism" or "non-dual mysticism"),[2] where God is fashioned in our human and cultural image and related to as a separate Being from humanity, a sort of Santa Claus figure who lives at the North Pole, is usually male, and is invariably quite judgmental and even punitive. This common and naïve image of God is actually the basis for much sincere atheism. Alone, this image of God is a straw man that can easily be blown away. And this is exactly why we must deal in a positive way with the issue it raises.

Many rightly feel that humanity has moved far beyond any "old bearded man sitting on a throne" kind of God, who always ends up looking like our past authority figures and who must be "feared," yet can also be cajoled into doing our will. This view seems to cheapen any honest or profound notion of God, and it surely has been subject to misuse and manipulation by immature people and clergy. These critics are, of course, half correct (God is surely not male nor a human writ large!), but I also believe their too quick and easy dismissal can also keep us from some wonderful possibilities and openings. Maybe God is *supremely* personal! But let's first define our terms.

In this chapter, I would like to offer my common "yes, and" approach (*sic et non* in medieval Catholic theology) to help Christians and unbelievers alike to know what is very good and deeply true about a personal notion of God, but then to move much further too. Francis surely loved and related to God as "Jesus" in a personal and intimate way, and yet he also saw God in "Brother Wind and Air," as "Sister Water," "Brother Fire," and "Sister, Mother Earth." *When you get to the more mature levels of mystical union everything becomes a metaphor for the divine, and you grab for metaphors to concretize the mystery that is now in everything and everywhere!* Interestingly, he composed his "Canticle to the Creatures" in Clare's garden while she was trying to nurse him back to health. It is hard to imagine that she was not some of its inspiration, she who herself loved to see all things as mirrors.

A Brief History of the Notion of a "Person"

The word *person* as we use it today, meaning a separate human individual, is not really found in the Hebrew Bible, but the idea of "face" is. Hebrew authors looked for a word to communicate the effect of "inter-face" with their Yahweh God who *seemed to want to intimately communicate with them:* "May God let his face shine upon you, and may his face give you peace" (Numbers 6:25–26). In the Greek translations, the noun used for face was *prosopon*, which literally referred to the stage masks that Greek actors wore, which seemed to serve as both an enlarged identity and a megaphone. This same usage is also found in several Psalms (42:2; 89:15–16; and 95:2), where it is often just translated as *presence*, meaning, more precisely, *communicated presence*—or a transference of selfhood from one to another.

The word *person* is also rare in the New Testament; one of the few times it appears, it is again translated as face. Paul says, "It is the God who has said, 'Let light shine out of darkness,' that has shone in our hearts to enlighten them with the knowledge of God's glory, the glory that is on the face (*prosopon*) of Christ" (2 Corinthians 4:6). This same language is then beautifully built upon in the second and third centuries by teachers like Tertullian and in the fourth century by the Cappadocian Fathers to communicate how God could be both one and three at the same time. Each member of the Trinity was considered a *persona* (Latin for *prosopon) or "face" of God. There is slowly an evolution of meaning.* Each person of the Trinity fully communicated its face and glory to the other, while also maintaining its own "facial" identity fully within itself.

Each person of the Trinity "sounded through" (*per sonare*) the other, which is really a quite brilliant way to describe the Trinity, and how relationships and all ecosystems essentially work. *This theology about the very shape of God became over time a way to psychologically understand how human beings operate too!* We were soon called "persons" in the same way that God is a person—not the other way around. In other words, we are created in God's very capacity for love and communion. Thus, our later notion of a human individual came from the Latin word *persona*, which was first applied to the Trinitarian God. We were each *soundings through*—of something much more and Someone Else. We were each a stage mask, a face, receiving and also revealing our shared DNA, our ancestors, and our past culture. It became our very understanding of the ensouled human being or "person"!

We called the negative side of this phenomenon "original sin," which created problems of its own, but we know that Augustine was just compassionately trying to explain *the obvious fly in the ointment of all visible reality.* Modern psychology, brain studies, neurology, physics, and most sciences now confirm the very real imperfection we see in all things. This imperfection becomes in wise people a kind of "negative feedback loop" that ironically keeps them in a state *of necessary imbalance and growth*—which appears to be the very dynamic of ongoing life. What a surprise, and sort of a disappointment, for those of us who want to start, continue, and end in total perfection. Did it ever strike you that when we commonly say "I am only human," it almost always translates as "I am allowed to be imperfect." They are the same thing, I think.

We are indeed social animals, "soundings through," and much that we do is programmed and given from our past, which is both wounding and wonderful.[2] It is very humiliating but also quite liberating to know about this imperfection ahead of time. Science would now call it "chaos theory" or "the principle of indeterminacy." Growth is never a straight line forward.

Psychology and anthropology also came to see that the human person was—without exception—a unique manifestation of an always larger and shared reality. We, exactly like the Trinity, are *inter-beings*. We are also created by interface. An individual manifestation of our entirely *shared humanity* was eventually referred to as a "human person," but the meaning was turned around 180 degrees, making *a person a separate and autonomous individual instead of an inherent "shareability"!* That is the direction that the egocentric and private self always moves—toward separation and not toward union. And this movement toward false autonomy has flowered in the postmodern world in which we now live.

In both liberals and conservatives it takes different forms of autonomy. Liberals want to be personally and intellectually autonomous, while conservatives want their money, power, and country to be autonomous. In that sense, neither of them is the "human person" created in the image of God, but they try to self-create themselves—as if they could.

The fourth-century Cappadocian Fathers tried to communicate this notion of *life as mutual participation* by calling the Trinitarian flow a "circle dance" (*perichoresis*) between the three, or a "soundings through" of three *persons*, each being a mask of, and megaphone for, the larger whole. They chose another clever word from the world of theater and popular culture. Despite their attempts to communicate to the masses, for too many Christians the doctrine of the Trinity was just unfathomable, abstract, and boring theology that could be nicely shelved. It was not much more than a speculative curiosity or a mathematical conundrum (yet surely never to be questioned or denied by any orthodox Christian). We paid a big price by not taking the foundational template of Trinity seriously and even ignoring it.[3] It was almost made to order to demolish our dualistic thinking by the dynamic principle of three.

Ignoring something is probably worse than outright denying it, since in denying you at least struggle with it or give it a kind of importance.

Who Created Whom?

But this leads me to my major point here, and one that has many spiritual implications. It is not that we are persons and that we have anthropomorphically created God in our image. It is not that we try to piously think of God as personal, so we can talk to him, and love her (although that is also true), but, in fact, it is exactly the other way around. God is both face and interface, with an infinite capacity for meaning, depth, mystery, mutuality, and communication, and it is *we who are created in* this Divine design, and not the other way around.[4] This is, I sincerely believe, the absolute core of the Judeo-Christian revelation. So, both

Yahweh and Jesus are indeed the very essence of what we mean by being "personal." *This is not to deny that God is Transpersonal too—Energy, Life Itself, Formlessness, Consciousness, Ground of Being, Truth, Love,* and so forth. Probably our metaphors for the Holy Spirit as a dynamic flow, fire, water, and descending dove were given to us to keep this dynamism and movement alive.

We live, therefore, in an entirely personalized universe, and we are made for communion and relationship with everything. Why not call it "divine curiosity" or "awe before mystery"? If you are not intensely curious, open, and searching, then I doubt whether you are in deep touch with the One who continues to generate all of the "ten thousand things" that surround us. God is nothing if not endless imagination and creativity. Our official Franciscan motto invites us to the same place: "My God and All Things" (*Deus Meus et Omnia*).

The simple biblical phrase "Let *us* make humanity in *our* own image, in the likeness of *ourselves*" (Genesis 1:26–27, emphasis added) now takes on a whole new depth and meaning (note the plural forms of the three pronouns). God and humanity really are mutually compatible, and the Trinity is indeed the blueprint for all created reality, as science from atoms to galaxies now reveals. This is why so many Christian mystics were absolutely fascinated by God as Trinity, and why we should be too. Their inner intuition was absolutely correct, although they struggled to articulate it just as we still do and forever will. The doctrine of the Trinity should forever keep all God-talk humble and stuttering. Modern science is just backing us up with some very confirming voices today.

So our personhood makes it possible to understand and relate to the exact same personhood in God; we have a built-in capacity for the Divine (*capax Dei*). *We were created with an inherent capability and desire for connection, communication, intimate love, forgiveness, and mutuality.* It is our "natural law," actually our "first nature," and I think any good psychologist would back this up. Is it any surprise that most mass murderers and psychopaths are often extreme loners? And saints are always compassionate and connecting. Always.

PERSONAL AND TRANSPERSONAL

Mature believers eventually move toward a *transpersonal* notion of God as presence itself, consciousness itself, pure Being, the very Ground of Being, the force field of the Holy Spirit, God with us, and God in all things—and yet many of these very same people frequently find it helpful, if not necessary, to still relate to God through the intimate sharing of one trusting self to another. "Why not?" would be my only question. I believe it takes two to love—a giver and a receiver. You normally do not give yourself, fall in love with, or surrender to a concept, an energy, a force, or even to enlightenment. Persons love persons, and the brilliance of Judeo-Christianity is that it keeps the whole spiritual life intensely personal in this very rich sense. This is perhaps what differentiates Christian mysticism from Buddhist enlightenment, which would avoid any belief in a personal God or even avoid our whole preoccupation with metaphysics. This allowed Buddhism to pay attention to other important things than those that Christians usually fought about.

The problem got worse for biblical faith as we presently define personal in a very whittled-down, individual, and largely emotional way, thinking that "I," Richard, can have a private relationship with my private God—by myself. This is actually *anti-Gospel* which still takes many Catholic, Orthodox, and Protestant forms. In the common American phrase, "I must have a personal relationship with Jesus Christ as my own Lord and Savior." There is way too much "I" and "my" there, although I admit that for most it is probably the only way to *start*. But it is not a good way to continue. Staying at this individualistic level has led to the flourishing of things like racism, sexism, unjust tax codes, deprivation of voting rights, an excessive need for guns and security, class hatred, and love of war in the very American states that most identify as "Christian." This is rather hard to deny, so I do not need to name names. As the ancients said, "The corruption of the best is always the worst."

THE DIVINE NATURE

So where does this all lead us? Well, God surely cannot be *less* than what it means to be "personal," but probably personal to the millionth power. The Jewish tradition began to see—and allow—*Divinity as an endless and ingenious capacity for connection and communion*, which starts with Yahweh's creative and constant interface with the people called Israel. "Personal" in my definition means that *an actual give-and-take is somehow possible*, and believers are not merely interacting with an impersonal force, idea, law, or rule. In that sense, many Christians, in fact, do not really have a "personal" relationship with God at all! They relate to God as an "unchangeable law" that cannot be disobeyed without dire consequences and that, if obeyed, merits automatic rewards. *God is more like a handy ATM machine that permits both deposits and withdrawals than an interactive "personal" relationship that we call love.* It is the difference between God as an ego possession or a propositional statement—and God as a dynamic and living relationship that allows us to *matter* to one another.

The personal God revealed in both the Scriptures and the Perennial Tradition makes known a *divine nature that is seductive, self-disclosing, and immensely self-giving to those who are interested. This experience of "overflow" invites us into immense freedom, along with intimacy and real friendship.* Such a relationship deeply empowers anyone who engages with it. (If any relationship does not somehow empower you, it is not authentic or truly "personal.") *Love in its mature and full form always creates some level of equality between giver and receiver.* That may seem totally impossible with God, but that gap is exactly what is overcome by God being "personal," and is why the Christian notion of God's great self-emptying (*kenosis*) in a personal Jesus is such a huge gift to our humanity. *Jesus reveals that the give and take of human and divine is utterly possible precisely by him becoming personal. It is what Martin Buber, the great Jewish philosopher, brilliantly describes as the "I-Thou" relation- ship.[5] It was the Jews who first dared to think this way, starting with the patriarchs, prophets, and the Psalms, reborn in our time through teachers like Buber and Emmanuel Levinas, who gave moral centrality to "the face of the other."*

This respectful give and take is so humanizing (and divinizing) that anyone who has enjoyed it will know that this is "as good as it gets" and would never retreat from it. To consciously reject such relationality, once experienced, would be the exact meaning of sin, self rejection, or hell. (Of course, many do not seem to have experienced this, so they can hardly reject it and go to hell!) We can see the same emphasis on rela- tionality in non-Christian mystics like Rumi, Hafiz, Kabir, Rabia, the Baal Shem Tov, and all the Jewish patriarchs and prophets.

Critics are right when they say that whoever the Divinity is, God cannot be limited or known as an independent object for anyone's personal possession, manipulation, or mere use. To do so would be a misuse of the truly personal in favor of a mere instrumental or mechanistic understanding of relationship (the "I-it" relationship, according to Martin Buber). It is represented in much early stage religion, where prayer is to get God to give you what you want. Here people try to control and cajole God by various techniques, moralities, rituals, and prayer forms. This is indeed creating God in our image and likeness, and what so many atheists rightly react against, instead of the much bigger truth that we must hold out for—where God is instead creating us in God's own "image and likeness" (Genesis 1:26)—precisely as *appreciative interface.*

The biblical God refuses to be in any kind of an I-it relationship but *holds out for, and thus educates us in, the I-Thou encounter* (which alone should be called "personal"). An authentic life of prayer teaches you how to live trustfully inside of such an I-Thou world, which is the very meaning of worship, love, and a life of total gratitude. *Any attempt to relate to God in an I-it way (that is, as a cosmic ATM) corrupts and even destroys the divine encounter itself.* God is always known through vulnerability and mutual self-disclosure, and this will always lead to an encounter with *God as Goodness.* First, God is known as *sharing my very Being—and in that gracious sharing God is then known as Goodness itself.* How else could we know this experientially?

This deep realization is what differentiates the mystics from the mere Sunday pew Christians. The very shape of the gateway into God makes it very likely that you will always meet God as a Lover, and not as a mere judge. An overly defended person, or someone who is antagonistic or hateful, will try to push his "squareness" through the "round" hole of God, and it just won't work. Without love from our side, we just cannot know God (1 John 4:8). Only vulnerability and mutuality can meet, know, or enjoy God. That is biblical "personalism," and is at the heart of Francis and Clare's idealization of poverty and humility.

Franciscan Trinitarianism

Francis refused to be a "user" of reality, buying and selling it to personal advantage (the I-it relationship). In fact, that is what he vigorously reacted against, and why he granted personal subjectivity to sun, moon, wind, animals, and even death, by addressing them as brother, sister, friend, and mother. Maybe his seeing, which was both personal and contemplative, is what forced him out and beyond the production-consumption economy where most people find themselves trapped today. Francis grants all of reality, even elements and animals, an intimate I-Thou relationship. This could be a very definition of what it means to be a contemplative, which is to look at reality with much wider eyes than mere usability, functionality, or self-interest—*with inherent enjoyment for a thing in itself as itself.* Remember, as soon as any giving wants or needs a reward in return, you have backed away from love, which is why even our common notion of "heaven" can keep us from the pure love of God or neighbor! A pure act of love is its own reward, and needs nothing in return. Love is shown *precisely in an eagerness to love.* Please dwell on these things.

When you start with Francis and Clare, and then move on to Bonaventure, Anthony, Scotus, Angela of Foligno, and the many Poor Clare saints and blesseds, you see that they appear to be living inside of a set of relationships that they quite traditionally name "Father, Son, and Holy Spirit." But these experiences of communion are real, active, and involved in their lives, as if they are living inside of a Love-Beyond-Them-Which-Yet-Includes-Them. They are drawn into an endless creativity of love in wonderful ways that reflect the infinite nature of God. They seem to shout out gratitude and praise in several directions: *from a deep inner satisfaction (the indwelling Holy Spirit), across to the other (the ubiquitous Christ), and beyond what I can name or ever fully know (the formless Father).* If I would be honest, our Trinitarian mystics sometimes make me wonder if I am in on the full Mystery myself yet. Maybe that is the very effect they are supposed to have on us.[6]

In the Trinity, both God and love finally have a solid definition and description, and cannot ever be sentimentalized again.[7] If Trinity is the template for all creation, from atoms to galaxies, which now appears to be the case, then a water wheel (Bonaventure's metaphor for the Trinity) that is always outpouring in one direction is a very fine metaphor for God. *Giving and surrendered receiving are the very shape of reality.* Now love is much bigger than mere emotions, feelings, infatuation, or passing romance. The spiritual life becomes a kind of *dancing while standing still*—because your entire life is both a quiet, calm standing and simultaneously a fervent moving—but it feels more like *being moved*! Willingness has now taken the place of your previous willfulness, which never got you anywhere anyway.

With Trinity as the first and final template for reality, love is the ontological "Ground of Being" itself (Paul Tillich). It is the air that you breathe, as any true mystic discovers, consciously or unconsciously. You do not have to be able to describe this in any words to experience it. In fact, you can't. You can only live it. What seems like one-sided self-emptying is no loss anymore, and unilateral receiving is no longer a humiliation. These last two paragraphs might be my summary of Franciscan mysticism.

Healthy religion teaches you how mature relationship works, and this is why good religion greases the wheels of human evolution. Unhealthy religion allows you to try to manipulate God, and almost certainly you will try to manipulate your daily life in the same way. *How you do anything is how you do everything.* Any healthy notion of God must not be modeled on our own grasping, needy, fear-based, and manipulative relationships. Yet that has been much of the history of religion. It is no wonder that a God modeled after our smallness is so often the God that so many atheists have rightly rejected.

One has to honor the very basics of love itself to get inside of the Real Game, which is why Jesus *commanded* us to love. *The way you love other humans and the way you love God are almost certainly identical.* God has his work cut out for him in teaching and evolving our human capacity for love, which is exactly why Jesus says the second commandment is just "like the first" (Matthew 22:39). How you love and how you allow yourself to be loved by God is how you love in general! Thus a Franciscan worldview would always emphasize practical acts of love and service as the only evidence that you actually love God (1 John 2:9).

SUMMARY

For me, it really comes down to this: the individuals I know who are most genuinely happy and also fruitful for the world invariably relate to God in a way that is deeply personal, intimate, and almost conversational. Yet these same persons would be the first to admit and recognize that their personal God is also transpersonal, and "the one in whom we all live, and move, and have our being" (Acts 17:28), and, finally, beyond all names for God. God is humbly recognized as beyond any of our attempts to domesticate, understand, or control the Mystery. All names for God are "in vain."[8]

An alive believer, a "Holy Roller" singing her sweet hymns to her beloved Jesus, a simple servant of the poor, might not use my fancy words like force field, spiritual energy, Ground of Being, and so on. But she might much better dance this mystery with her feet, serve it with her arms, and flow into it with her tears than those of us who only talk about it. As Rumi so poetically puts it, "There are a thousand ways to kneel and kiss the ground."[9]

It is common, I am afraid, to have a very articulate, transpersonal, and orthodox theology, as I think I do, but not be inside the actual Flow at all, which will always feel quite personal, intimate, outflowing, and something like *Yes*. Good teaching is only to open doors and eliminate unnecessary obstacles, but most of you do not need to be teachers or articulators. You only need to remain inside the Flow—and unafraid to kneel and kiss the ground.

How Are Things "Caused"?

Poetry must resist the intelligence
Almost successfully.[1]

—WALLACE STEVENS

WISDOM, JUST LIKE GOOD POETRY, must and will always "resist intelligence," as New England poet Wallace Stevens says enigmatically. It gives just enough of reality to keep us out of our too-easy egotistic center and still needing more; and, quite honestly, needing a spiritual state to complete the "logic." Mature spirituality, or wisdom, insists that we hold out for meaning instead of settling for mere *answers*. Wisdom is necessarily and always partially hidden, and reveals herself only to those who really want her and will not try to make a commodity of her (Old Testament book of Wisdom 6:12–22; 7:22—8:8). It is the same with God.

I hope this appendix will give you many new possibilities for your understanding of mysticism, which is the highest form of wisdom.

Mysticism will not oppose your intelligence, but it will "resist" it, and then will expand your understanding far beyond the limits of a mere literalism, or mere physical notions of causality. Francis of Assisi, in particular, is a wholesale assault on cultural logic and how things change and are changed, how things grow and grow up.

Even correct ideas and church mandates cannot effect the kind of change that the soul needs; the soul needs living models to grow, and quite precisely exemplars with the expansive energies of love. *People who are eager to love change us at the deeper levels; they alone seem able to open the field of both mind and heart at the same time.* (Pre-marriage counseling is often the most fruitful and effective of all. It is probably the only time many males are willing to talk at depth without a major problem to solve.) When we are in this different state, and that is what it is, we find ourselves open to directions or possibilities we would never allow or imagine before or after.

TYPES OF CAUSALITY

When I studied Scholastic philosophy we had an extended course on "causality." We learned that there were formal causes of things, material causes, efficient causes, final causes. Each was carefully defined, but the one that especially intrigued me was called an "exemplary cause." With that kind of causality, someone or some event, just by being what it is, by being an example or model, "causes" other things to happen as a result (just as truly as a strong arm might cause a rock to be dislodged from a field, which would be called the "efficient cause"). Our understanding of *what causes what*, just like poetry, must also resist "too quick intelligence." Only then can we read situations in much larger and more helpful frames.

After Newtonian physics emerged, most people thought efficient causes were the only way that things could happen, but a wise person should know differently. This entire book hopes to present Francis as an exemplary cause of a whole bunch of things, almost all very good. "Final causes" then work in much the same way, but from the other end, *by pulling us forward through attraction and allurement.* Final causes "cause" things to emerge and evolve in a certain way by offering ideals, models, and seductions that pull us forward. One's destiny or goal (*telos*) finally determines one's meaning, as Bonaventure teaches. If your end goal is clear to you, you have your North Star for a coherent life purpose. It will quite truthfully pull you forward and give you a clear trajectory, for good or for ill. It is your final cause.

When I taught in Africa, again and again I heard how Nelson Mandela initiated an evolutionary leap forward for many African males, especially when they saw pictures of him hoeing in the fields, which was still considered women's work. He is a good example of both an exemplary and a final cause. He changed the tangent and the possibility for many people. I still find this understanding of causality rather brilliant and important, and a much needed liberation from the Western imprisonment inside of the literal cause and effect model of Newtonian physics.

Most fundamentalist Christians are still imprisoned inside of a very limited understanding of how things are "caused," and it has thus severely limited their theological understanding of things like miracles, grace, sacraments, the teachings of the Bible, salvation, evolution, forgiveness, and Jesus himself. Some well-known TV evangelists rejoiced that sinful New Orleans was being punished by God with Hurricane Katrina, even after Jesus clearly said things did not work that way (Luke 13:2–5). In fact, such a mechanistic worldview makes many such things understandable only at a very childish, often cruel, and really untrue level ("first-tier consciousness" in Spiral Dynamics). Instead of a living, loving Trinity, we have a fearsome *deus ex machina,* "God as a machine."

These different forms of causality prepare you to examine Scripture, tradition, and your own experience in a very mature way.[2] Our Living School at the Center for Action and Contemplation seeks to make *experience itself something solid and trustworthy,* and not the "mere subjectivity" that Western Catholics and Protestants have too easily dismissed.[3] Both exemplary and final causes come close to what Karl

Jung means by an archetype or archetypal energy.[4] Paul himself has this very understanding of both Adam and Christ, as "types" (*tupoi*) or "prefigurements" of the universal human patterns (Romans 5:14–19).

Adam, Paul says, "caused" sin and Christ "caused" grace, but it does no good whatsoever to understand this in a simplistic and mechanical way. It diverts attention from the same patterns in ourselves, which such archetypes are intended to point us toward (the "adam" in me, the "christ" in me). As always, we worship the archetype instead of participating now in the same truth ourselves; and "Christ" ends up *taking our power instead of giving it to us*—which is his desire and plan. We did the same with the sacraments by understanding them in terms of mechanical and efficient causality ("*ex opere operato*," so called) instead of personally transforming encounters in ways that could be at least partially evident.

Exemplary causality knows that your mother did "cause" you to be the person you are by being the person that she is, or that your father or your grandfather's occupation has operated as a final cause for your whole life's trajectory. Causality takes on a whole new depth and breadth when we recognize the many ways that *this* causes *that*, and we can never again revert to fundamentalist Christianity (which actually demands very little faith but insists on certitude and answers) as a cheap substitute for the great biblical notion of faith. Literalism is a well-hidden form of rationalism, and a severe limit on God's possibilities and freedom for creative action. Every time we honor a hero, paint a good icon, or canonize a saint, we are allowing that person to be both a final and exemplary cause of very good things happening in our world, precisely *because of raising them up as a symbol and ideal.* (Some are saying that Pope Francis is effecting more attitudinal change in the Church in a few months than all of the documents of Vatican II.)

Try to appreciate the Christ as the exemplary cause of salvation in the sense of an Alpha Point, "hidden plan" (Ephesians 1:9, 11) or "blueprint" from which all creation moves forward (Scotus), and then also the final cause, the Omega Point toward which all history is being drawn, just as the book of Revelation said in several places (1:8; 21:6; 22:13). The beginning and the end create the trajectory forward in a clear direction. Then the incarnate Jesus holds history on course by personally exemplifying its concrete manifestation as the "New Man" (Ephesians 2:15) or the "Perfect Man" (Ephesians 4:13) in a chosen moment of time. O*ne person, symbol,* or *prime idea* can very definitely set the course of history and its meaning in one direction instead of another.

We recognize this in some celebrities and public figures who "turn" history, art, music, and politics in new and unimagined directions, as I said above about Nelson Mandela and Pope Francis. Picasso did this for art, Michael Jackson did the same for body movement and dance, and Einstein did it for physics and the universe. You cannot even imagine something or do something—until you can first have an *image* of it inside you, which is surely why Einstein said that "imagination is more important than intelligence" (and he, of all people, earned the right to talk that way!).

Jesus, our greatest exemplary cause, modeled the whole human journey, from divine conception, to ordinary looking life, to rejection, cross, resurrection, and ascension. He symbolically—but really—walked the journey first, and thus directed and eased the path for those of us who could now know life's inevitable direction and certain outcome. He gave history an *ontological basis for hope* (which is far deeper than mere psychological or temperamental "hopefulness"). Jesus is the complete and sufficient package for those who want it, and it might be one way of describing how Jesus "saves us." (This is also central in a full understanding of Adam and Eve, Abraham and Sarah, Moses, Melchizedek, Job, Mary, and the Cosmic Christ, who are each archetypes and stand-ins for much larger realities. Reading the text this way is called the *typological* level of interpretation, and without it, it is very hard, as I said before, to understand what Paul means when he says we "die in Adam" or we "live in Christ." We just glaze over, as we do with so many Scriptures if we reduce them to mere literalism.)

If you are limited to efficient or formal causalities, you will think in a mythical and magical way, which is the first-tier thinking that many associate with religious people. If you stay there, you will remain trapped in one small tribe and outside of any active, attractive, or compassionate faith. After the Enlightenment and the creation of Newtonian physics, we went backward spiritually, and started to understand all causality only in physical and efficient ways (which does not do justice to how reality fully works, as even field theory and family-systems theory now make very clear). The world itself—as well as people's inner and prayer lives—then became arid and mechanical instead of juicy and enchanted. Soon God was indeed "dead," as was the soul.

This limited view of causality is unfortunately why so many educated people have abandoned what they think is the Christian explanation of reality. They know God is not a cosmic puppeteer, although much of our vocabulary and most of our hymns seem to imply just that. Many people, especially young people who want to be "authentic," start feeling phony and withdraw from what seems to them like such a crude and manipulative worldview. *Immature Christianity is primarily responsible for the vast agnosticism we now see in the Western world.* I have little doubt of that. In my experience, a more subtle and honest naming of how God humbly, slowly causes things (*grace* is the word here) tends to draw sensitive people back into the Christian drama, often with great excitement and gratitude. God does not like to live in the spotlight, but is revealed only through indirect light, so only the sincere seekers find love and grace and freedom.

Understanding exemplary and final causes is so much more satisfying and helpful an explanation than the one most Christians settle for, spiritual explanations that feel like juridical transactions, such as: Jesus needing to "pay a price" to change the mind of God; sacraments that "automatically dispense" grace like a vending machine; Jesus as the one who "forever destroyed death" when we still see death all around us. It seems so artificial and contrived to outsiders, as though God has been made to fit inside of our infantile minds. Such a God often becomes literally "unbelievable" to a sincere but well-developed adolescent brain. I have met them for forty years. People normally have no need to react against God; it is only our arrogant, cruel, and glib ideas about God that they are usually rejecting. As Christian Wiman puts it, "We find the fire of belief fading in us because the words are sodden with overuse and imprecision.... They no longer burn."[5] My desire in writing this book is to allow good words to burn again in your heart.

IMAGINAL CAUSALITY

In recent years, through the teachings of Cynthia Bourgeault on Mary Magdalene, this notion of the importance of symbol and corporate personalities helped me understand how our imaginal world operates and changes us.[6] Bourgeault helped me to see that *imaginal* is not *imaginaria*. Each of our *imaginaria*—our unconscious but operative worldview, constructed by our experience, including all the symbols, archetypes, and memories that inhabit it—are foundationally real and have very concrete effects. Jews, Catholics, Hindus, Franciscans, and Protestants all live in quite different *imaginaria*, and there is not much point in calling another one "wrong."

We each understand or respond to our own *imaginarium*! (To not recognize that is probably what it means to be a narcissistic personality.) Catholics get so upset when they hear of Buddhists who have apparitions of the Buddha—and not Jesus! And, of course, Mary only appears to Catholics, which certainly shows we have the true Christian faith! But God can only come to any of us in images that we can trust and believe, and that open our hearts. God is that humble, it seems to me.

Cynthia Bourgeault carefully distinguishes the many women named Mary in the New Testament and concludes, along with others, that in a very real way they are all the same person.[7] In actual *effect*, there is only one archetypal Mary, and she is always *receptive and trusting*. She is always saying, "Let it be!" Maybe the New Testament writers, and the Holy Spirit, were much smarter than we thought and left it intentionally ambiguous so it could operate on the unconscious. (*Too conscious* can often mean *self-conscious*—and thus very open to control by the ego.)

For many Christians, the very word "Mary" evokes an entire *imaginarium* in the soul, and it then does its very real work. All of the Marys exercise a transformative, "bridal mysticism" on the human psyche. They feminize, sweeten, give *eros* and pathos to the spiritual journey. They exercise one foundational imaginal causality, but in a hundred ways—according to how, when, why, and with what readiness we read the text or look at the image. A heart open to the power of good metaphor, open to the feminine, and open to intimacy, will leap every time. A heart trapped in historical literalism, or closed to the power of the feminine, will remain bored, reactive, and trapped in critique. (The active dislike and mistrust some evangelicals have for Mary defies Scriptural or rational analysis.)

Archetypes can really change us at a deep level if we can allow them access, but we have wasted much time trying to perfectly distinguish and explain each of the Marys, and then feel a need to prove our point of view as the only correct one. The quiet trust and confidence that "Mary saves," which felt like Catholic overstatement or bad theology, was on one level entirely true (at least for Orthodox and Catholics anyway). But that is only because Catholics have a very different *imaginarium* than the typical Protestant. I guess Mary cannot easily "save" Protestants, but only because they won't let her.

On the level of soul, there is only one Eternal Mary Symbol, who is both real and archetypal, and she is doing Jesus's work from the feminine side as the *Magna Mater*. As Jesus is the archetype of the Divine Gift Itself and how the Gift is Given, so "Mary" is the archetype of how the Divine Gift is Received, and she makes it quite clear that the Gift must always be received in our "lowliness" (Luke 1:48, 52). Now, the ego does not like to consider itself "hungry" (Luke 1:53) or "lowly," which is exactly why the ego remains such a "hungry ghost." The soul draws its riches and its food from these very depths, and darkness becomes its own kind of light. This is the preferred language of most mystics.

Plato, later Neo-Platonists, and, in our time, Carl Jung, recognized that the shared imaginal world is where encounter and deep change really happen. In the end, it is more real and effective than something that is *not* shared in the imaginal world. (Now I know why it has been said that the whole history of Western philosophy is merely a series of footnotes to Plato.) The lovely four-seasoned cottonwood tree outside my window is indeed physically real, but until you or I take it into our imagination, take it seriously, focus on it, allow it to stir us, it really has no lasting or real effect on our lives. It is the imaginal world that changes us and steers history more than the naked existence or nonexistence of the physical tree. That is what fundamentalists and atheists refuse to understand, and it is why good poets and mystics will change us much more than unenlightened physicists or bad theologians.

How Grace Might Just Work

My grand point in bringing imaginal causality up at the end of the book is that I wholeheartedly believe that this is the way spiritual life and spiritual truth is transferred. There is little point in continuing to argue over whether any biblical event happened in a precise way or at a historical moment. That kind of literalism will seldom be major or life-changing. It is largely a waste of time, although I would never deny that there are real historical foundations in the Bible, and that similar things can surely happen in our history—as long as we keep our interpretations spiritual and open-ended, and thus transformative. *Transformation and personal encounter are the whole point, the power, and the possibility of religion*, and not the rather empty and useless concern with "Did it really happen just that way?" Instead, we must ask "How does it still happen that way now?" That can bear fruit, and fruit that will last.

For example, it really does not matter to me whether there was a fig tree (Mark 11:13–21), whether Jesus cursed it or not, whether it withered or not, or even what his exact original point was (How could he expect us to know any of that?). If we can get beyond these superficial arguments, we can, in fact, hear an important but hard critique about the unfruitfulness of externalized religion, which the context makes rather clear. By allowing ourselves to be sidetracked by such argumentative and rational questions, we have lost centuries of needed wisdom and the possibility for changed lives and world. *Literalism is the lowest and least level of meaning.* Sacred stories, and honest ritual, imaginally cause the same things that happened in Scripture to happen again—even for us—and even now.

If we can believe that Jesus apparently cares about feeding the hungry by his many "multiplication" of bread and fish stories, then we can also conclude that God cares about feeding the hungry today, and that we also should be multiplying food, as he did, to make this possible. Just saying "Wow, Jesus is a true wonderworker!" or "This proves he is God!" does not help the reader, the world, the hungry, or the transformative power of the Gospel (it should be unnecessary even to have to say this, it is so obvious).

Hindus and Buddhists and Confucians seem to know this way of interpreting reality more than the three "Religions of the Book": Judaism, Christianity, and Islam. We each got trapped inside of our bookish books, where words are first of all differentiating and describing, which is their good purpose. The trouble is that this solidifies us in dualistic thinking as a substitute for the experience itself. This is exactly what the Jewish people were trying to overcome by "re-presenting" the founding event through *ritually re-membering it* in later space and time, as they do with the Passover Meal, and Catholics do with the Eucharist, and Muslims do with sacred pilgrimages. We were all trying to move beyond words to actually changing peoples' *imaginaria* at the unconscious level, where real change must first happen. *If your inner imaginarium is rich, intelligent, and not overly defended, you will never stop growing spiritually.* Read more poetry, literature, and mythology, would be my advice. Then we can trust you with the Scriptures and the saints.

FRANCIS AND CLARE AS IMAGINAL CAUSES AND EXEMPLARS OF HOLINESS

Just as Pope Francis exercised a worldwide and major imaginal change in the year 2013, amazingly sped up by the World Wide Web and social media, Francis and Clare have done for eight hundred years in the Christian world. They told us by their lives that Christianity could be joyful, simple, sweet, and beautiful. Our spiritual intuition got it, and many us have found that our psyches shifted too—although largely on the unconscious level of possibility. Even art shifted, as we see in Giotto, eventually leading to the Renaissance where the human could be honored and celebrated as good in itself. Francis and Clare rearranged our imaginal world, apart from any single word or idea that they spoke. Remember that most of the power of imaginal causality is at the level of soul, where we do not consciously know it is happening. And therefore we cannot engineer it, do not need to understand it, nor can we fully stop it! Yeah!

If we "perfectly understand" how God is changing us, if we try to be too rational about it, we will only fight grace, try to personally steer the soul (dangerous!), and, of course, take argumentative sides (which is what we have largely done). *God works best underground, by rearranging our assumptions and presuppositions and dreams—frankly, when we are asleep, and not in control,* exactly as the psalmist promised (127:2). How else could God gain control in this ego-driven world of ours? Most grace and healing happen "secretly," not in the very moment when you pray for it or are prayed over. Then God alone gets the credit, and we are free from our pushing, claiming, using, inflating, and manipulating.

I believe that the Gospel itself, and the Franciscan vision of the Gospel, is primarily communicated by highly symbolic human lives that operate as Prime Attractors: through actions visibly done in love; by a nonviolent and humble, simple, but liberated lifestyle; by a happy identification with the poor and the excluded of the world; by obvious happiness itself; and by concrete and visible people who "give others reasons for spiritual joy"—as Francis said when he rubbed two sticks together to play his own imaginary violin and as Pope Francis did when he washed the feet of prisoners, women, and Muslims. When such people then speak or act, *their words burn and their actions convict!*

Surely this is what Jesus meant when he told us to "shout the message from the housetops" and to be "a light on a lampstand," or to be "leaven" and "salt." He knew that holiness is passed on through *contagion*, and from inside, and seldom by simple, "correct matter and form," or any juridical criteria for *validity* as most Catholic and Orthodox priests were trained in sacrament class.[8] Transformed people transform people. Francis and Clare were quite simply transformed people—who still continue to deeply change us today.

Without knowing it, Francis was directly teaching imaginal causality when he is quoted as saying, "You must preach the Gospel at all times, and when necessary use words." He knew that happy and humble people finally change people, much more than ideas, sermons, or theology ever will. We must know that any encounter with a large or lovely life changes our imagination forever. We always henceforth know it is really possible. We are thus attracted forward.

We all know love's absence as hell, and its presence goes by the name of heaven. We all know the difference intuitively and energetically between people who are in heaven now and people who are in hell now. This demands no "belief" or theology whatsoever, but only open eyes that mirror God's eternal eagerness to love, and the imaginal world that such eyes create within us.

A man like St. Francis of Assisi, for instance. What does
he really mean?... A complete break with the pattern of
history...a man born out of due time. A sudden, unexplained
revival of the primitive spirit of Christianity. The work he
began still continues...but it is not the same. The revolution is over. The revolutionaries have become conformists.
The little brothers of the Little Poor Man are rattling alms
boxes in the railway square or dealing in real estate to the
profit of the Order.... Of course, that is not the whole story.
They teach, they preach, they do the work of God as best
they know, but it is no longer a revolution, and I think we
need one now.[1]

—MORRIS WEST

I HOPE THIS BOOK CAN help reignite the Franciscan revolution, for that
is what it was—and will be again. We are extremely blessed to be living
in the time of a pope who most beautifully exemplifies what I am trying
to say in this book—and even more—because it is so much harder to
do in our time. Pope Francis shows us that the Franciscan vision is

possible at every level and in every age. Not only did he take the name Francis; but he seems *so eager* to proclaim both the "foolishness" and the wisdom of the Gospel to every level of society. He has the passion, love, and urgency of Francis himself, and has moved the papacy from the palace to the streets.

Both Francises—pope and saint—reveal our slowness and deep resistance to living the actual life of the Beatitudes and the Sermon on the Mount. Yet the whole world is thrilled when it sees someone dare to actually live it! As Pope Francis says in his courageous and first apostolic exhortation, "The Joy of the Gospel," "Let us not allow ourselves to be robbed of the Gospel!"[2] If the Holy Spirit indeed guided Pope Francis's election, which I surely believe, then it appears that God is also pushing for this continuing revolution of the Gospel that Morris West so hoped for in 1963 when the Second Vatican Council was just beginning. God is surely very patient.

Among the many things I try to say in this book, I hope these reflections will help us recognize one helpful truth: *There is a universal accessibility, invitation, and inclusivity in an authentic Franciscan spirituality.* It surpasses the boundaries of religion, culture, gender, ethnicity, era, class, or any measure of worthiness or education. Like the Incarnation itself, the Franciscan reading of the Gospel "brings everything together, in the heavens and on the earth, behind Christ who is leading the way, and in whom we are all claimed as God's own" (Ephesians 1:10–11).

This is not an elitist journey, not a separatist or clerical journey, not a journey based in asceticism or superiority, but a journey based in the elements that are universally available to all humans: nature itself, embodiment, solidarity with the necessary cycle of both life ("attachment") and death ("detachment"), the democracy of love, and most especially with a God "who is very near to you, in your mouth, and in your heart" (Deuteronomy 30:14). This is what divine grace is—always given—unawares and unearned and everywhere, but sadly too often unwanted.

The Franciscan alternative way is alternative precisely because it names, gathers, suffers, and transforms what is already happening all of the time. There is no group to join here, no physical body to reject, nor anyone to exclude. As the last chapter of the Bible reminds us, we are already floating—all of us—in this immense and gracious "river of life, rising from the throne of God, already flowing crystal clear down the middle of the city streets" (Revelation 22:1–2).

You see, only love can move across boundaries and across cultures. Love is a very real energy, a spiritual life force that is much more powerful than ideas or mere thoughts. Love is endlessly alive, always flowing toward the lower place, and thus life-giving for all, like a great river and water itself.

When you die, you are precisely the capacity you have developed to give and to receive love. *Your recognition of this is your own "final judgment" of yourself, which means you become responsible for what you now see (not shamed or even rewarded, but just responsible).*

If you have not received or will not give this gift of love to others, your soul remains tied to a small, earthly, empty world which is probably what we mean by *hell*. (God can only give love to those who want it.)

If you still need to grow in love and increase your capacity to trust Love, God makes room for immense growth surrounding the death experience itself, which is probably what we mean by *purgatory*. (Time is a mental construct of humans. Why would growth be limited to this part of our lives? God and the soul live in an eternal now.)

If you are already at home in love, you will easily and quickly go to *the home of love which is surely what we mean by heaven*. There the growth never stops and the wonder never ceases. (If life is always change and growth, eternal life must be infinite possibility and growth!)

So by all means, every day, and in every way, we must *choose* to live in love—it is mostly a decision—and even *be eager to learn the ever deeper ways of love*—which is the unearned grace that follows from the decision!

Then I can only end with Pope Francis's plea and question from "The Joy of the Gospel": "So what are we waiting for?"[3]

NOTES

FRONTISPIECE

1. Ken Wilber, *One Taste: Daily Reflections on Integral Spirituality* (Boston: Shambhala, 2000), p. 100.

PREFACE

1. Neale Donald Walsch quote found, among other websites, at http://soul-essence.com/2011/10/. I find much of his work quite compelling and helpful.

2. Thomas of Celano, "First Life of St. Francis," in Marion Habig, O.F.M., ed., *St. Francis of Assisi: Omnibus of Sources* (Cincinnati: Franciscan Media, 2009), p. 318.

3. Immediately after I wrote this first paragraph, I opened to this telling passage, which I took as confirmation of this "one spiritual truth" in Francis: "Often, without moving his lips, he would meditate within himself. He drew external things within himself, and they would lift his mind to even higher things." Thomas of Celano, "Second Life of St. Francis," *St. Francis of Assisi: Omnibus of Sources*, p. 440.

4. Bonaventure, "The Breviloquium," *The Works of St. Bonaventure* (St. Bonaventure, N.Y.: St. Bonaventure University Press, 2005), p. 253.

5. Christian Wiman, *My Bright Abyss: Meditation of a Modern Believer* (New York: Farrar, Straus and Giroux, 2013), p. 92.

6. "Legend of Perugia," *St. Francis of Assisi: Omnibus of Sources*, p. 1088.

7. Regis J. Armstrong, *Francis of Assisi: Early Documents*, vol. 3, *The Prophet* (New York: New City, 2001), especially the General Introduction, and André Vauchez, *Francis of Assisi: The Life and Afterlife of a Medieval Saint* (New Haven, Conn.: Yale University Press, 2012), pp. 324–336. This fine biography represents the newer, more critical kind of biography that is taking the place of the longstanding pious and legendary lives of Francis, which only makes him more inspiring.

8.   Jon M. Sweeney, *Inventing Hell: Dante, the Bible, and Eternal Torment* (New York: Jericho, 2014). I recently wrote a very supportive blurb for this book that has been a long time in coming. With solid scholarship, Sweeney makes clear that our contemporary notion of a punishing God has been much more formed by *The Divine Comedy* of Dante than by the actual teaching of the Bible. This negative imagery has done untold damage in both making people fear God—and fear that God does not actually practice what he preaches! With that doubt and fear, most people will never get to the mystical level of Christianity.

CHAPTER ONE

1.   Gregory Orr *Concerning the Book that is the Body of the Beloved* (Port Townsend, Wash.: Copper Canyon, 2012), p. 29.

2.   I will stand by my definition of mysticism, although I have much appreciated and learned from the more scholarly ones by Evelyn Underhill, William James, and Bernard McGinn. I encourage you to learn more from them in their more extensive studies of mysticism.

3.   I was first confronted with the immediate and long-lasting effects of "the Baptism in the Spirit" on November 8, 1971, when a group of resistant young teenage boys suddenly began to sing in tongues and spent the whole night in chapel after a sermon I gave on the prodigal son. It not only changed their lives, it also changed mine and eventually many others. It became the New Jerusalem Community in Cincinnati. Only when my mother later reminded me did I remember I had been ordained in Topeka, Kansas, on the exact spot where the Pentecostal movement began in 1901. See also Wolfgang Vondey, *Pentecostalism: A Guide for the Perplexed* (New York: Bloomsbury T&T Clark, 2013), and Larry Martin, *The Topeka Outpouring of 1901* (Joplin, Mo.: Christian Life, 2000).

4.   By dualistic thinking, I mean the common untrained way of seeing everything in binary splits as good or bad, with me or against me, etc. Contemplation makes you capable of non-dual thinking, where you stop splitting and dividing

the field of the moment between what you like and what you don't like. My book *The Naked Now: Learning to See as the Mystics See* is entirely devoted to this crucial understanding (New York: Crossroad, 2009).

5.   St. Francis of Assisi, "Testament," *St. Francis of Assisi: Omnibus of Sources*, p. 68.

6.   Could being *closed down* be the core and essential meaning of "sin"? I was taught that sins "offended God"—as if we could! I believe Divine Love is so perfect that it is only "offended" when we act against our own depth and best interest, just as a good parent laments and pities the foolish choices of their child. Paul can hardly tell us "love takes no offense nor does it store up grievances" (1 Corinthians 13:5), and then find out God's love is less mature than ours. God cannot possibly be *personally offended* as such, just as our True Self cannot be offended. When the Holy Spirit sees God's own creation self-destruct, that is what the Spirit surely "grieves over" (see Ephesians 4:30). When we close down, we are choosing death over life, and that is indeed "mortal" sin, because God, who always wants more life for us, can no longer get through.

7.   Ilia Delio, *A Franciscan View of Creation: Learning to Live in a Sacramental World* (St. Bonaventure, N.Y.: Franciscan Institute, 2003). As always, Ilia gives us the good theology to undergird such an opinion.

8.   Richard Rohr, *Immortal Diamond: The Search for Our True Self* (San Francisco: Jossey-Bass, 2013). This is the major point of chapter five, "Thou Art That," the classic Hindu phrase that, in its own verbiage, has been rediscovered by many authentic mystics.

9.   I mean by the term True Self, and the reason I capitalize it, one's objective, metaphysical, and unchangeable identity as a child of God. Many of us would understand this in distinction to the "false self," which is created by psychological and passing influences, although this is sadly the self with which most people identify. Religion's job is to help the false self to "die" so the True Self can be "found," to use Jesus's frequent advice.

10. Eloi Leclerc, O.F.M., *Wisdom of the Poverello* (Chicago: Franciscan Herald, 1961), p. 79. A poetically written meditation based on Francis's trials and actual life.

11. Auspicius Van Corstanje, O.F.M., *Francis: Bible of the Poor* (Chicago: Franciscan Herald, 1977), and *The Covenant with God's Poor* (Chicago: Franciscan Herald, 1966). This Dutch friar illustrated the real scriptural significance and universal message for Francis's love of poverty and littleness.

12. Thomas of Celano, "Second Life," chapter 84, 120.

13. From his song "Anthem," at http://www.leonardcohen.com/us/music/futureten-new-songs/anthem.

14. G.K. Chesterton, *Life of St. Francis.*

CHAPTER TWO

1. Johann Baptist Metz, a Catholic theologian and professor emeritus of fundamental theology at Westphalian Wilhelms University in Münster, Germany, is the author of a small book, *Poverty of Spirit* (Mahwah, N.J.: Paulist, 1998) which has become a bit of a classic. It was the very last book I read before I went home to Kansas to be ordained, and I knew it was to be essential in my understanding of priesthood.

2. I was very happy to see that the new group of cardinals, gathered around Pope Francis, has used the term *authority* in precisely this way. They are saying that church authority is the ability to "author" life in others, and not the exercise of dominative power, which is secular authority. It has taken us a long time to come to this rather clear teaching of Jesus.

3. Rohr, *Immortal Diamond*, especially chapter two.

4. St. Bernardine of Siena, Works II, Sermon 60.

5. Bonaventure, "Major Life of St. Francis," *St. Francis of Assisi: Omnibus of Sources*, p. 732.

6. Read the four amazing, graphic descriptions of a "Servant to Suffering," who would reveal the very shape of liberation for the world, in Isaiah 42:1–9; 49:1–7; 50:4–11; and 52:13—53:12. These passages provide a lifetime of

meditation on how God works in such an upside-down way and might just reveal the summit of biblical prophecy.

7.   Jürgen Moltmann, *The Crucified God* (New York: Harper & Row, 1974). This courageous, creative, and contemplative study on the meaning of the cross is a book that foundationally influenced my entire understanding of Christianity and Jesus. It will lead you far beyond any mere "substitutionary atonement theory."

8.   Van Corstanje, O.F.M., *Francis: Bible of the Poor* (or *The Covenant with God's Poor?*).

9.   I talk about these as "the Four Splits" in *Immortal Diamond*, pp. 29ff.

10.   Pope Francis, *Evangelii Gaudium*, 222. Here the Holy Father offers a central principle that "Time Is Greater than Space." A mature Christian should initiate *processes* that bear fruit in the long run instead of merely holding and defending one's own space, role, and power.

CHAPTER THREE

1.   Regis J. Armstrong, *Francis of Assisi: Early Documents,* vol. 2, *The Founder* (New York: New City, 2000).

2.   Albert Gelin, *The Poor of Yahweh* (Collegeville, Minn.: Liturgical, 1964). A common prophetic theme (Zephaniah 2:3; 3:12) is that only a humble remnant—those at the bottom—will fully get the message of salvation. Many strains of liberation theology in the 1980s returned to the same insight. Read Gustavo Guttiérrez, Jon Sobrino, and Leonardo Boff, who were all enlightened by the poor of Latin America. Mary sums up this biblical attitude in her "Magnificat" (Luke 1:46–55).

3.   Richard Rohr, "Spiral of Violence: The World, the Flesh, and the Devil" (Albuquerque, N.M.: Center for Action and Contemplation, 2008), CD recording on the classic sources of evil. This point is hard to deny when you note how almost no one goes to jail for bank failures or massive white collar crime, and very few in the military system are prosecuted for sexual assault. These are our recent examples of patriarchal power, and to most people it just looks normal. Evil can hide in systems much more than in individuals.

4.   St. Francis of Assisi, "Testament," *St. Francis of Assisi: Omnibus of Sources*, p. 67.

5.   Thomas of Celano, "Second Life of St. Francis," *St. Francis of Assisi: Omnibus of Sources*, p. 102.

6.   Richard Rohr, *Breathing Under Water: Spirituality and the Twelve Steps* (Cincinnati: Franciscan Media, 2011), chapter five. This utterly important distinction between God's way of "justifying" reality and the human juridical way is crucial for the Church and penal systems if they are to rediscover their unique roles in society.

7.   Pope Francis, *Evangelii Gaudium*, 232.

8.   Rohr, *Breathing Under Water*, especially the introduction.

9.   *Eight Core Principles* (Albuquerque, N.M.: Center for Action and Contemplation, 2012).

10. Richard Rohr, "Emotional Sobriety," CD (Albuquerque, N.M.: Center for Action and Contemplation, 2012).

CHAPTER FOUR

1.   Thomas of Celano, "First Life of St. Francis," *St. Francis of Assisi: Omnibus of Sources*, p. 296.

2.   Thomas of Celano, "Second Life of St. Francis," *St. Francis of Assisi: Omnibus of Sources*, pp. 494–495.

3.   Bonaventure, "The Journey of the Soul to God," I, 9 (New York: Paulist, 1978).

4.   Thomas of Celano, "Second Life of St. Francis," *St. Francis of Assisi: Omnibus of Sources*, p. 495.

5.   Dawn M. Nothwehr, O.S.F., *Franciscan Theology of the Environment* (Cincinnati: Franciscan Media, 2003). This book is the best single resource and collection for much that I am trying to say in this chapter.

6.   "Legend of Perugia," *St. Francis of Assisi: Omnibus of Sources*, pp. 1055–1056.

7.   Illuman is the name of the men's organization that was spawned from my early work with men. Visit Illuman.org for information about dates and places for male initiation rites, etc.

8. Roger D. Sorrell, *St. Francis of Assisi and Nature: Tradition and Innovation in Western Christian Attitudes toward the Environment* (New York: Oxford University Press, 1968), pp. 142ff.

9. Ewert Cousins, *Bonaventure: The Soul's Journey to God* (New York: Paulist, 1978). Chapters one and two have us start with the sensory world of things, chapters three and four lead us to trust our inherent capacity called soul, and chapters five and six lead us into pure Being and Goodness themselves, which we would call God.

10. Cynthia Bourgeault, *The Holy Trinity and the Law of Three: Discovering the Radical Truth at the Heart of Christianity* (Boston: Shambhala, 2013), p. 72.

11. On my last day of church history class in 1969, the final words of my Franciscan history professor, who had taught us for four years and well-prepared us for this shocking statement, were these: "Remember, the Christian church was probably more influenced by Plato than by Jesus!" We knew it was sadly and tragically true.

12. André Cirino and Josef Raischl, eds., *Franciscan Solitude* (St. Bonaventure, N.Y.: St. Bonaventure University Press, 1995), pp. 214ff. Almost every major Franciscan reform proceeded from a return to hermitages (life primarily in solitude instead of community) and ever-new discoveries of forms of prayer or depths of prayer, including the early Capuchins. It is also surprising how many of our friar saints were hermits before they joined the community, or moved away from community into *retiros* or solitudes.

13. Lawrence Landini, O.F.M., "The Causes of the Clericalization of the Order of Friars Minor" (Chicago: Gregorian University, Rome, 1968). Larry Landini was my teacher when his groundbreaking doctoral thesis was published, and it exercised a major influence on many of us in returning to our "laybrother" beginnings and foundation. We are friars first, and some of us are priests secondarily. Priesthood for us is merely a role and function that gives us greater access to the people, and that makes a big difference, even though it carries a lot of dangers with it. I do think this approach distinguishes "Franciscan"

priesthood from many others, although some brothers' communities, like the
Marianists, have discovered the same thing.

14. G.K. Chesterton, *St. Francis of Assisi* (New York: Dover, 2008), chapter six.

15. Thomas of Celano, "Second Life of St. Francis," *St. Francis of Assisi: Omnibus of Sources*, p. 211.

16. Documents of the Second Vatican Council, Decree on the Appropriate Renewal of the Religious Life, *Perfectae Caritatis*, 2.

CHAPTER FIVE

1. Much of the present pro-life movement and the American Tea Party might be examples of groups that have an important core of truth but present it with such an angry, dualistic, narrow, or righteous energy that it overrides their initial message and then becomes their de facto message—and soon gathers other people with that same level of negative energy. It thus becomes "ugly morality," yet on moral high ground. This would be the opposite of a contemplative or truly Christ-like morality. Only those with the ability to "discern spirits" (1 Corinthians 12:10) can tell the subtle but crucial difference between the two. This charismatic gift of the Spirit is at the heart of what we mean by wisdom.

2. Legend of Perugia, 43.

3. Mary Oliver, "Her Grave," *Dog Songs* (New York: Penguin, 2013), p. 29.

4. Rohr, *Immortal Diamond*. This is the core message of this entire book, and really my only message in all of my books: Humans enjoy an inherent, God-given connection with God, and that changes everything. See also Olivier Clément, *The Roots of Christian Mysticism: Texts from the Patristic Era with Commentary* (London: New City, 2002). This book is a masterpiece of collected sources largely unknown in the West.

5. I find Ken Wilber's clear distinction between *stages* and *states* very helpful here. One can be at a higher psychological/cultural/historical *stage* of evolution, but still live in a quite dualistic *state* (educated but antagonistic people, much of the postmodern world). Whereas one can be at a non-dual *state* of

consciousness, but still be at a mythic or magical *stage* of consciousness, which helps you understand how some saints could have aspects of anti-Semitism or even be warlike, as were John of Capistrano and Joan of Arc (personally loving and holy, but still trapped in their own moment of limited culture). Even Jesus seems to illustrate this stage when he calls the Syro-Phoenician woman a "dog" (Mark 7:27). Thank God, he catches himself and apologizes.

6. Rohr, *The Naked Now*. This is the message of this book from the historical, theological, and psychological levels. In my book *Everything Belongs: The Gift of Contemplative Prayer* (New York: Crossroad, 2003), I distinguish the contemplative mind from the "calculating mind," which is our normal but egotistic way of thinking from the reference point of the small self.

7. Richard Rohr, *Falling Upward: A Spirituality for the Two Halves of Life* (San Francisco: Jossey-Bass, 2011), especially the introduction.

8. Bonaventure, *Itinerarium*, 3, 2; Augustine, *De Trinitate* (Collected Works), 14, 8, 11.

CHAPTER SIX

1. Vauchez, *Francis of Assisi*, pp. 289, 292.

2. "Legend of Perugia," *St. Francis of Assisi: Omnibus of Sources*, p. 74.

3. source?

4. Landini, "The Causes of the Clericalization of the Order of Friars Minor."

5. Vauchez, *Francis of Assisi*, pp. 324ff.

6. The Fraticelli ("Little Brethren") or "Spiritual" Franciscans were extreme proponents of the Rule of Francis, especially with regard to poverty, and regarded the wealth of the Church as scandalous. They were thus forced into open revolt against some church authority and were declared heretical in 1296 by Boniface VIII (who was not very orthodox himself).

7. Vauchez, *Francis of Assisi*, pp. 200ff.

8. As I wrote this on August 2, 2013, the feast of the Portiuncula, the Franciscans are making our 804th rent payment to the Benedictines for their "little portion" of land. I wonder what would happen if the Benedictines ever demanded it back? We would find out if we "own" it.

9. Bourgeault, *The Holy Trinity and the Law of Three*. This important book will help you rediscover many corollaries that proceed from our basic template of the doctrine of the Trinity, and why two is inherently antagonistic until you introduce the reconciling third. Plato had already said the same in his "Principle of the Triad," *Timaeus* (31 B.C.): "It is impossible that two things should be joined together without a third. There must be some bond in between them both to bring them together." It sounds like a strong premonition of what we Christians call the Holy Spirit.

10. Richard Rohr with John Feister, *Hope Against Darkness: The Transforming Vision of Saint Francis in an Age of Anxiety* (Cincinnati: Franciscan Media, 2001), pp. 109ff. This was my first attempt to communicate Francis's Third-Way approach.

11. Thomas of Celano, "Second Life of St. Francis," *St. Francis of Assisi: Omnibus of Sources*, p. 397.

12. *St. Francis of Assisi: Omnibus of Sources*, Admontion 20. St. Bonaventure says that Francis said this constantly.

13. St. Francis of Assisi, "The Writings of St. Francis," *St. Francis of Assisi: Omnibus of Sources*, pp. 57–64.

14. St. Francis of Assisi, "The Writings of St. Francis," *St. Francis of Assisi: Omnibus of Sources*, pp. 65–70.

15. Vauchez, *Francis of Assisi*, p. 105.

16. Once Pope Gregory IX in his 1230 bull *Quo Elongati* declared that the "Testament" of Francis had no juridical value, we applied that juridical approach to everything. If the pope does not "require" it of us, it must not be important! The whole Church did much the same thing with a lot of Jesus's teaching. "If you cannot measure it or enforce it, it is not really required or significant," we think.

17. Thirteenth-century Scholastic theology itself proceeded by asking the *questio*, and refining the *questio*, and then alternative answers were accepted, as we see in Peter Lombard's famous *Sic et Non*, which held sway among scholars for

three to four centuries. Our very word *quest* comes from this non-fundamen-
talist approach to discussing the mystery of God. After the sixteenth century,
we all gradually moved on to the *defensive stance*, and needed to be totally right
and to prove others totally wrong—sadly ending up becoming rather *offensive*
ourselves in the process. See my *The Naked Now*, chapter six.

18. "A friar is not bound to obey if a minister commands anything that is contrary
to our life or his own conscience" is in chapter five of the Rule of 1221 ("The
Writings of St. Francis," *St. Francis of Assisi: Omnibus of Sources*, p. 35), with a
slightly different formulation in chapter ten of the Rule of 1223. This is in no
way typical in the thirteenth century; it is, in fact, quite revolutionary.

19. *Evangelii Nuntiandi*, 41.

20. Because I am not a scholar or an academic, I offer you some scholarly sources
which will discuss my theses of an alternative orthodoxy much better and
with more authority than I can here. I hope this can help you see that these
are not just my ideas, but are well represented inside the orthodox, Franciscan,
and Perennial Tradition of Christianity. The Franciscan way is radically traditional, which ironically ends up making it look quite radical. These scholars
are doing for Franciscan studies what twentieth-century biblical scholars did
for our more critical and more faithful understanding of Scripture: They are
giving us an underlying hermeneutic so we can interpret texts inside of a critical and historical context. See *The Franciscan Heritage Series* (St. Bonaventure,
N.Y.: Franciscan Institute, n.d.), and *The History of Franciscan Theology*, edited
by Kenan B. Osborne, O.F.M. (St. Bonaventure, N.Y.: Franciscan Institute,
2007).

CHAPTER SEVEN

1. Paraphrased from "Letter to a Minister" in Regis J. Armstrong, *Francis of
Assisi: Early Documents*, vol. 1, *The Saint* (New York: New City, 2000), p. 97.

2. Thomas of Celano, "Second Life of St. Francis," *St. Francis of Assisi: Omnibus
of Sources*, pp. 481–482.

3. One Scripture scholar pointed out to me that whenever Luke uses the word *crowd* or its equivalent in his Gospel, it is a code word for those who will have the wrong opinion or have missed the point.

4. Richard Rohr, *Adam's Return: The Five Promises of Male Initiation* (New York: Crossroad, 2004), pp. 92–104. I take initiation to be whatever phenomenon, ritual, or reality that leads a person into the awareness of inner presence, divine mystery, or transcendence. It does not have to be an opening into "religion," but it will always somehow be an initiation into "Spirit" and the reality of the spiritual world.

5. Michio Kaku and Jennifer Trainer Thompson, *Beyond Einstein: The Cosmic Quest for the Theory of the Universe* (New York: Random House, 1995), pp. 111–112. I heard Michio speak at two different science and consciousness conferences, and he is an excellent example of how the line between mystical religion and great science is becoming very slim indeed, yet he uses almost no directly religious language as such.

6. Thomas of Celano, "Second Life of St. Francis," *St. Francis of Assisi: Omnibus of Sources*, pp. 481–482, 196.

7. Rohr, *Falling Upward*, chapter three.

8. Spiral Dynamics and Integral Theory are two names for recent attempts to chart the development of consciousness. I find both of them very helpful and true to my limited experience. Writers such as Clare W. Graves, Ken Wilber, Don Beck, Robert Kegan, and Jean Gebser will all give you different takes on this very helpful understanding.

9. St. Francis of Assisi, "The Writings of St. Francis," *St. Francis of Assisi: Omnibus of Sources*, p. 62.

10. Rohr, *Breathing Under Water*.

11. Quoted in Christian Raab, Harry Hagan, eds., *The Tradition of Catholic Prayer* (Collegeville, Minn.: Liturgical, 2007), p. 121.

12. Joseph F. Schmidt, F.S.C., *Walking the Little Way of Thérèse of Lisieux: Discovering the Path of Love* (Frederick, Md.: The Word Among Us, 2012), pp.

135ff. Despite all of the attempts to sentimentalize this modern saint, Brother Joe Schmidt has the ability to show how rigorous and real her "science of love" really is. Thérèse for me is an archetype of what a saint should be: not a seeker of heroic martyrdom or ascetical anything, but one committed to the perfection of the art of loving both God and neighbor. Her "little way" is as close to a contemporary rediscovery of Francis's "integration of the negative" as I can find, and especially so because she brings an everyday psychology and interiority to what can still be seen in external "poverty" terms in Francis and Clare. She was a Carmelite who, almost on her own, rediscovered the Franciscan impulse, and thus she calls it "new," which for most of us it clearly is.

13. Scott Peck personally told me that he believed this line from Thérèse was enough to show her psychological and spirtual genius. He said the same in his book *People of the Lie*.

14. Rohr, *Falling Upward*, pp. xviii–xxix.

15. Quoted in Thomas Gilgut, *A Spiritual Guide for Today: The Path to Real Happiness* (Indianapolis: Dog Ear, 2010), p. 15.

16. Richard Rohr, "The Art of Letting Go: Living the Wisdom of Saint Francis" (Boulder, Colo.: Sounds True, 2010), six CDs on this theme.

17. Richard Rohr, "Francis: Turning the World on its Head: Subverting the Honor/Shame System," CD (Albuquerque, N.M.: Center for Action and Contemplation, 2008), recorded webcast.

18. Quoted in *Newsweek*, Volume 113, p. 105.

19. Chris Ellery, "The Nativity of John the Baptist," printed with his permission.

CHAPTER EIGHT

1. Quoted in Arthur L. Clements, *Poetry of Contemplation: John Donne, George Herbert, Henry Vaughan and the Modern Period* (Albany, N.Y.: State University of New York, 1990), p. 51.

2. Jacques Dalarun, *Francis of Assisi and the Feminine* (St. Bonaventure, N.Y: Franciscan Institute, 2006), pp. 127–154.

3. Vauchez, *Francis of Assisi*, pp. 309ff.

4. This is simply my way of saying it, and we can find many better ways, or you can surely disagree with mine and find clear exceptions to these general "principles." But that very need and mindset, and even determination to "prove wrong," or what I call dualistic thinking, is what I mean by being overly masculine, which also characterizes many women, and is also absent in many men. We are speaking of inner/soul *principles* here, not gender identifications, and it is also one way to describe the deep complementarity and paradox that is found at the core of sexual attraction, all biological reproduction, and even language itself.

5. Karl Stern, *The Flight From Woman* (New York: Paragon, 1965), pp. 140ff.

6. Bill Plotkin, *Nature and the Human Soul: Cultivating Wholeness and Community in a Fragmented World* (Novato, Calif.: New World Library, 2008). Bill and I have taught together, and he presents incarnational spirituality in a quite unique and compelling way.

7. Leonardo Boff, *Saint Francis: A Model for Human Liberation* (New York: Crossroad, 1984), chapter one.

8. Jordan of Giano, *Chronicle: XIII Century Testimonies* (Chicago: Franciscan Herald, 1961), chapters eight and twenty-four.

9. Arnaldo Fortini, *Francis of Assisi* (New York: Crossroad, 1992). This is one of the most helpful and truly informative biographies because Fortini gives us access to the actual social, political, economic, and religious history of Francis and Clare's lifetime. It was a time of nonstop violence, incessant class struggle, and records show that his father was indeed a very greedy man. It explains a lot about Francis's radical response, which previously had been merely romanticized.

10. These healing socio-dramas of Jesus were offered in two different settings. First, there is the bread-and-wine meal that was a ritual of healing, forgiveness, and community, based on the Passover meal, which some call the Lord's Supper, and which promises his "Real Presence." The second, the largely forgotten bread-and-fish meal, is depicted at least as much in Scripture as the

bread-and-wine meal. The bread-and-fish meal seems to have been a potluck to feed the poor and include the outsider, although it also was subject to abuse (1 Corinthians 11:17–22). The elders, who came to be called priests, soon took over the bread-and-wine meal, while "mere deacons" were in charge of the second (Acts 6:1–4), and it was then lost over time, as was the washing-of-the-feet ritual (see John 13:14–15, where he seems quite clearly to make it a sacrament). You can draw your own connections. But surely our selective attention was drawn toward focused sacralization, containment of "Presence," and a very real elitism—and away from anything ordinary, inclusive, and egalitarian. That is what patriarchs are almost always afraid of, as are any matriarchs who are upwardly mobile.

11. The rest of this chapter is taken from the unpublished bachelor's thesis I wrote in 1966 to distinguish Franciscanism from the older monastic forms of religious life, which I tried to show were much more patriarchal in their structure, and even their image of God. They merely reflected their period of emergence in Christian history, whereas Francis was centuries ahead of his time.

12. Erich Fromm, *The Art of Loving* (New York: Harper, 1956), pp. 67ff.

13. Fromm, pp. 67ff.

14. "Legend of the Three Companions," *St. Francis of Assisi: Omnibus of Sources*, pp. 948–949.

15. St. Francis of Assisi, "The Writings of St. Francis," *St. Francis of Assisi: Omnibus of Sources*, p. 40.

16. St. Francis of Assisi, "The Writings of St. Francis," *St. Francis of Assisi: Omnibus of Sources*, pp. 72ff.v(emphasis added.)

17. St. Francis of Assisi, "The Writings of St. Francis," *St. Francis of Assisi: Omnibus of Sources*, p. 37.

CHAPTER NINE

1. Regis J. Armstrong, *Clare of Assisi, The Lady: Early Documents* (New York: New City Press, 2006).

2. Marco Bartoli, *St. Clare: Beyond the Legend* (Cincinnati: Franciscan Media, 2010). I waited for such a book for a long time and was not disappointed. Bartoli succeeds in putting Clare in her real historical and cultural context, and making her radical faith and virtue all the more prominent.

3. Bartoli, *St. Clare,* chapter three on "Courtesy" and chapter nine on "War and Peace" both illustrate that Francis and Clare intentionally "changed social classes" at great cost to themselves and with great resistance from their families. Poverty was not just a private virtue for them, but a change of solidarities and loyalties, with clear social implications.

4. Vauchez, *St. Francis of Assisi*, pp. 292–296.

5. Bartoli, *St. Clare, Beyond the Legend*, p. 114.

6. Armstrong, "Third Letter to Agnes of Prague," *Clare of Assisi, Early Documents*, p. 51.

7. Armstrong, *Clare of Assisi, Early Documents*, p. 51.

8. Armstrong, "Fourth Letter to Agnes of Prague," *Clare of Assisi, Early Documents*, p. 55.

9. Armstrong, *Clare of Assisi, Early Documents*, pp. 55–56.

10. Rohr, *The Naked Now*, pp. 105ff.; *Everything Belongs; Immortal Diamond.* This has been the core message of several of my books, but is made much clearer by the recent teachings of John Main, Thomas Keating, Cynthia Bourgeault, and Laurence Freeman.

11. St. Teresa of Ávila, *Vida*, chapter four.

12. Not sure where this is even hinted at in any of the Gospels? They got caught up in thirteenth-century cultural expectations of women, I am afraid. It was probably the Christian form of the Moslem burka, and creates the same mystique.

13. Darleen Pryds, *Women of the Streets: Early Franciscan Women and their Mendicant Vocation* (St. Bonaventure, N.Y.: Franciscan Institute, 2010). This is a fascinating study of the entirely different context in which women had to live in the thirteenth and fourteenth centuries in Catholic Europe.

14. Rohr, *Falling Upward*, chapter nine.
15. Pope Alexander IV, "Clare Claris Praceclara" (#4 in Franciscan Historical Archives, #13 in Latin).
16. Wilber, *One Taste*, p. 85.
17. Ingrid J. Peterson, O.S.F., *Clare of Assisi: A Biographical Study* (Quincy, Ill.: Franciscan, 1993), p. 347.
18. Clare's final recorded words in the earliest accounts.

CHAPTER TEN

1. Thomas of Celano, "Second Life of St. Francis," *St. Francis of Assisi: Omnibus of Sources*, p. 388.
2. Kathleen Warren, *In the Footsteps of Francis and the Sultan: A Model for Peacemaking* (Rochester, Minn.: Sisters of St. Francis, 2013); Paul Moses, *The Saint and the Sultan: The Crusades, Islam, and Francis of Assisi's Mission of Peace* (New York: Doubleday, 2009); George Dardess and Marvin L. Krier Mich, *In the Spirit of St. Francis and the Sultan* (Maryknoll, N.Y.: Orbis, 2011).
3. One wonders if there is any connection between the Crusades and the separation between Rome and Constantinople in 1054. The East became our estranged brother and even our "enemy," which on some levels has lasted to this day.
4. Thomas of Celano, "The Second Life of St. Francis," *St. Francis of Assisi: Omnibus of Sources*, p. 389.
5. Thomas of Celano, "The Second Life of St. Francis," *St. Francis of Assisi: Omnibus of Sources*, p. 388.
6. Rule of 1221, *St. Francis of Assisi: Omnibus of Sources*, p. 47.
7. Richard Rohr and Andreas Ebert, *The Enneagram: A Christian Perspective* (New York: Crossroad, 2001), pp. 14ff. I am personally convinced that Blessed Raymond Lull, who perhaps encountered Sufi "schools of spiritual direction" and surely the Jewish Kabbalah, was trying to find a hearable common *vocabulary* between Christians, Muslims, and Jews, and an "enneagram type" tool gave him that neutral but spiritual language he hoped all three religions could

respect. His nine names for God and nine virtues are listed on pages 16–17 and correlate rather well with the Enneagram's notion of nine major virtues and vices.

8.   Thomas of Celano, "The Second Life of St. Francis," *St. Francis of Assisi: Omnibus of Sources*, p. 389.

9.   St. Francis of Assisi, "The Writings of St. Francis," *St. Francis of Assisi: Omnibus of Sources*, pp. 43–44.

CHAPTER ELEVEN

1.   Bonaventure, "Sermon for the First Sunday of Lent" *The Works of St. Bonaventure* (Patterson, N. J.: St. Anthony Guild, 1960).

2.   Étienne Gilson, *The Philosophy of St. Bonaventure* (New York: Sheed and Ward, 1938), p. 494.

3.   Cousins, *The Soul's Journey to God*, 7, 6.

4.   Bonaventure, *The Works of St. Bonaventure, Hexaemeron*, 3, 2 (Paterson, N.J.: St. Anthony Guild, 1960).

5.   Denis Edwards, *The God of Evolution: A Trinitarian Theology* (New York: Paulist, 1999). This would be one example of the present convergence between physics and theology, and even Trinitarian theology. Denis Edwards, an Australian priest and scholar, has a number of fine books that explore these ideas at length. I highly recommend any of them. See also John Polkinghorne, *Science and the Trinity: The Christian Encounter with Reality* (New Haven, Conn.: Yale University Press, 2004), which is equally wonderful.

6.   Ewert Cousins, *Bonaventure and the Coincidence of Opposites* (Chicago: Franciscan Herald, 1978).

7.   Ilia Delio, O.S.F., *Simply Bonaventure: An Introduction to His Life, Thought, and Writings* (New York: New City, 2001), p. 12 and throughout. Delio also agrees with Cousins's coincidence of opposites as a central theme, and the cross itself as a "mandala" of transformation.

8.   Cousins, *The Soul's Journey*, I, 14.

9.   Rohr, *Immortal Diamond*. My attempt to do this often takes the form of clarifying what we mean by our True Self and the false self. We must begin with

"identity theology" before we dive into moral theology or salvation theories or we never work our way back to our core identity.

10. Landini, especially pp. 138–142.

11. Moses, *Francis and the Sultan*, pp. 5–6, 197ff.

12. George H. Tavard, *From Bonaventure to the Reformers* (Milwaukee: Marquette University Press, 2005).

13. Cousins, *Bonaventure and the Coincidence of Opposites*, pp. 255ff.

14. Zachary Hayes, O.F.M., *The History of Franciscan Theology* (St. Bonaventure, N.Y.: Franciscan Institute, 2007), chapter two. Hayes offers the best single summary on Bonaventure's thought that I have read. Bonaventure both teaches and exemplifies non-dual consciousness.

CHAPTER TWELVE

1. Thomas M. Osborne, Jr., *Human Action in Thomas Aquinas, John Duns Scotus, and William of Ockham* (Washinton, D.C.: Catholic University of America Press, 2014), p. 104.

2. Ken Wilber, *A Brief History of Everything* (Boston: Shambhala, 1996), pp. 19ff, and throughout Wilber's work, from Arthur Koestler's term to describe something that is simultaneously a "whole and a part." Benoit Mandelbrot did approximately the same with what he called "fractals" in 1975.

3. Mary Beth Ingham, *Scotus for Dunces: An Introduction to the Subtle Doctor* (St. Bonaventure, N.Y.: Franciscan Institute, 2003). This is the accessible and very readable text for our generation, as so much of Scotus is still in Latin and, even when translated, sometimes hard to follow, his thinking is so "subtle" and rarefied.

4. We know so little about Scotus's personal life, but his commitment to the big picture and the common good reveals he had moved beyond egocentricity and tribal thinking to cosmocentricity, yet *he brilliantly transcends but also includes the individual*. I am drawing upon the analysis of Ken Wilber's Integral Theory and many other developmental theories, who all tend to agree that we grow in this direction: egocentric>soulcentric>cosmocentric. The biggest task is getting people out of "first-tier" egocentricity.

5. Wiman, *My Bright Abyss,* p. 121.
6. I once had the privilege of meeting with the Scholastic philosopher Josef Pieper, at the Indian dances at Santo Domingo Pueblo, New Mexico, on August 4, 1969, and he told me he had written this in one of his books. I overwhelmingly agree with it.
7. Richard Rohr, *Things Hidden: Scripture as Spirituality* (Cincinnati: Franciscan Media, 2008), chapters seven through nine especially deal with the biblical issues that led to the substitutionary atonement theory.
8. Richard Rohr, *From Wild Man to Wise Man: Reflections on Male Spirituality* (Cincinnati: Franciscan Media, 2005), especially chapters on the "father wound" and "father hunger."
9. Rohr, *Breathing Under Water,* pp. 21ff., on the "myth of sacrifice."
10. Gerard Manley Hopkins, "Duns Scotus' Oxford," *Poems and Prose* (New York: Penguin, 1985), p. 40.

CHAPTER THIRTEEN

1. Wiman, *My Bright Abyss,* p. 23. One of the most profound books I have read in recent years, even if not an easy read. I keep going back to its incarnational wisdom.
2. Thomas of Celano, "The First Life of St. Francis," *St. Francis of Assisi: Omnibus of Sources,* pp. 254–256.
3. "Little Flowers," *St. Francis of Assis: Omnibus of Sources,* p. 1322.
4. Paul Tillich, *A History of Christian Thought* (New York: Simon and Schuster, 1967), p. 182.
5. George Weigel, *Tranquillitas Ordinis: The Present Failure and Future Promise of American Catholic Thought on War and Peace* (New York: Oxford University Press, 1987).
6. Alfred North Whitehead, *Science in the Modern World* (New York: Macmillan, 1925), p. 223.
7. Among the many developmental schemas that have emerged in the last century, I find many of them converging in the stage conceptions of Clare

Graves and Chris Cowan called "Spiral Dynamics," and the "Integral Theory" of Ken Wilber. I cannot begin to do them justice here, although I do my own simple application to the world of spiritual direction in the nine stages listed in Appendix I in the book *The Naked Now*.

8. Rohr, *Falling Upward*. This is the building of the container that we must do in the first half of life, but is not yet the contents that the container is created to hold.

9. Adolf Holl, *The Last Christian* (New York: Doubleday, 1980), pp. 1ff. This controversial biography of Francis still deserves far more attention than Christians and Franciscans have been willing to give it.

10. Rohr, *Immortal Diamond*, preface, especially p. xxi.

11. Wiman, *My Bright Abyss*, p. 121.

12. Wiman, *My Bright Abyss*, pp. 21ff.

13. Rohr, *Everything Belongs*. A distinction between "calculative knowing" and "contemplative knowing" is much of the point of this book. Contemplation is an alternative form of consciousness that we must now be taught "consciously" because it is no longer natural to our overstimulated and agenda-driven cultures.

14. Nancy K. Morrison and Sally K. Severino, *Sacred Desire: Growing in Compassionate Living* (West Conshohocken, Penn.: Templeton, 2009). These two doctors—neighbors of ours here in Albuquerque—make clear the very neural foundations for love and holiness. In her new publication, *Behold Our Moral Body: Psychiatry, Duns Scotus, and Neuroscience* (London: Versita, 2013), Severino makes a brilliant connection between Duns Scotus and the findings of modern neuroscience. I happily wrote the foreword for the book.

APPENDIX I

1. Rohr, *Immortal Diamond*. My original intention in writing this book was to try to correlate the many Scriptures on this new presence that the first Christians called the Risen Christ. It led me to see that the Risen Jesus is the divine presence beyond any confines of space and time. The Eternal Christ

has now appeared in a personal form that humans came to know and love as "Jesus." Now the Resurrection is not so much a miracle, certainly not a resuscitation, as it is an apparition of what *has* always been true and *will* always be true.

2. Richard Rohr, *Great Themes of Paul: Life as Participation,* CD (Cincinnati: Franciscan Media, 2000), audio presentation. Many Christians do not like or understand Paul, whom you cannot appreciate unless you also share to some degree in his non-dual love of both the historical Jesus *inside of* the larger and eternal Christ. Mind boggling, once you notice this.

3. Amos Smith, *Healing the Divide: Recovering Christianity's Mystic Roots* (Eugene, Ore.: Resource, 2013). I happily wrote the afterword for this fine study, because I think Smith restores the dynamism needed in our understanding of the two natures of Christ. We lost it and must still regain it.

4. Ilia Delio, *Christ in Evolution* (Maryknoll, N.Y.: Orbis, 2008), *The Emergent Christ* (Maryknoll, N.Y.: Orbis, 2011), and *The Unbearable Wholeness of Being* (Maryknoll, N.Y.: Orbis, 2013). Delio, a Franciscan sister and theologian, has the ability to take solid tradition and make it very contemporary and even revolutionary, as it always should be. Teilhard de Chardin is the great prophet here, but few foresaw his importance.

5. Rohr, *Immortal Diamond*, chapter six, especially the first definition of *catholic* by St. Vincent of Lerin in 434.

6. Clément, *The Roots of Christian Mysticism.* This masterpiece deserves to be known. It combines both original sources and profound commentary on the early Church fathers, who still understood and taught divinization, but they were mostly in the East, so we stopped talking to them, and they stopped influencing us, after the Great Schism of 1054. Western seminaries never exposed clergy to this wisdom, so it comes like a huge surprise to most of us.

7. Richard Rohr, "The Divine Dance," CD (Albuquerque, N.M.: Center for Action and Contemplation, 2006), audio presentation. My feeble attempt to bring out the wonderful soul- and mind-expanding implications of God as Trinity.

8. "The Church that existed since Abel," the first victim, whose sacrifice pleases God, is a very intriguing and telling phrase that was used by St. Augustine, St. John Damascene, St. Gregory the Great, and then quoted in the Second Vatican Council's *Lumen Gentium*, 2. Obviously the formal church had not yet been founded, but all those whose victimhood "cries out from the earth" to God (Genesis 4:10) are already the eternal mystery of the Church.

9. Wiman, *My Bright Abyss*, p. 67.

APPENDIX II

1. Adapted from Kahlil Gibran, *The Prophet* (New York: Alfred A. Knopf, 1923), p. 55.

2. By speaking of formless or non-dual mysticism, I am referring to people who do experience radical union with Reality or Mystery, but do not necessarily use the word God, or give this God a specific personal name. Deity mysticism is usually personal and gives God a name and image. All of the monotheistic religions opened the door to formless mysticism: Judaism, by the warning against speaking God's name; Christianity, by keeping both the Father and the Holy Spirit without an image; and, Islam by forbidding the painting of divine images. Yet they do not reject God as a "person," and, in fact, introduce and affirm this very idea.

3. David Brooks, *The Social Animal: The Hidden Sources of Love, Character, and Achievement* (New York: Random House, 2012). A very well-written and engaging book by a true conservative, which is sure to take away some of our hubris about being "self-made" or being humans capable of perfect intellectual certitude about "facts."

4. This is a necessary conclusion from the Christian doctrine of the Trinity, which gives shape to all things. "The Divine Dance" audio presentation came from me and "The Shape of God" audio presentation with the partnership of Rev. Cynthia Bourgeault (both available from the Center for Action and Contemplation, Albuquerque, N.M.). If you get the Trinity, and you can get beyond your anti-Christian prejudices, you can get the big pattern of Reality—and at its foundations.

5. Martin Buber's classic *I and Thou* is available in many editions. I consider it one of the most important books I ever read, not just to understand the biblical revelation, but to understand human relationships too. For this Jewish philosopher and wise man the "I-it relationship" is the common functional and opportunistic way of relating that is necessary for most daily exchanges. As is, it is neither bad nor good, but just necessary. The much higher "I-Thou relationship" is revealed in the very nature of many languages that have two forms of the second-person address. The first is the generic "you" and the second is for people that you wish to honor with intimacy, specialness, or dignity. It is curious that *thou* died out in the English language, except in prayers, and now has died out there too.

6. I would like to offer for your prayer a Litany of the Holy Spirit that I composed during one long hermitage experience in 2007. It offers sixty-five metaphors for God, which are all invitations for divine engagement and encounter—through personal, energetic, conceptual, poetic, physical, and theological images (*The Naked Now*, appendix 3, pp. 168–169). If even one of these opens up your inner space, as they did mine during that time, I will be very happy.

7. Catherine Mowry LaCugna, *God for Us: The Trinity and Christian Life* (San Francisco: HarperSanFrancisco, 1991). Many consider this to be the best systematic study of the doctrine of the Trinity in our time. Without some Trinitarian notion of God, personal in the sense we have defined it here, both an internal and always outpouring Love, it seems we always return to an old and tired image of God—and then react against it. (The Latin word for God, *Deus*, came from the Greek god Zeus, who was mostly known for throwing thunderbolts. Most cultures return to some such patriarchal image if they do not have an open-ended mystery, like Trinity, which both veils and reveals the Mystery at the same time.)

8. Rohr, *The Naked Now*, chapter two, pp. 25–26. The sacred name Yahweh must not be spoken, and can only be "breathed" in and out!

9. Helen Buss Mitchell, *Roots of Wisdom: A Tapestry of Philosophical Traditions* (Stanford, Conn.: Cengage, 2010), p. 310.

APPENDIX III

1. George S. Lensing, *Wallace Stevens and the Seasons* (Baton Rouge, La.: Louisiana State Unversity Press, 2004), p. 151.

2. "Scripture as validated by experience, and experience as validated by Tradition, are good scales for one's spiritual worldview" is the first methodological principle of the Rohr Institute Living School (see cac.org).

3. Wiman, *My Bright Abyss*, p. 27. I find that poets and mystics have a strongly developed capacity for discerning their inner experience, somewhat as Wiman describes it here: "Our goal should be to acquire and refine a sense of consciousness that is capable of registering the most minute changes in sensation, feeling, faith, self. Unless we become aware of the transitions that are occurring all the time within us, unless we learn to let experience play upon our inner lives as on a finely tuned instrument, we will try to manufacture inner intensity from the outside." I think Wiman has named a crucial reason for our present cultural decline, addiction, and emptiness. We are a totally extroverted culture, and even the introverts have little guidance for interpreting their inner worlds. Thus, most of us do not really *experience our experiences, much less allow them to change us at deep levels.*

4. An archetype is an inner "ruling image" that is largely non-rational and operates unconsciously. You either get it on the subliminal level or you don't. If you do, it has its strong effect. If you don't, it is harmless and ineffective.

5. Wiman, *My Bright Abyss*, p. 124.

6. Cynthia Bourgeault, *The Meaning of Mary Magdalene: Discovering the Woman at the Heart of Christianity* (Boston: Shambhala, 2010), pp. 61ff.

7. Bourgeault, *The Meaning of Mary Magdalene*, pp. 25ff.

8. A bishop once questioned whether Jesus was really present at a Eucharist I celebrated because the mother of the groom baked the tortillas I consecrated for a wedding Mass (almost identical to the bread Jesus would have used, and surely the food of the poor—and, here in New Mexico, surely holy bread too). "Check if she used salt or baking soda," he told me! If so, he would have to

doubt the validity of the Mass (and therefore apparently the marriage?). He really believes this because his *imaginarium* is entirely different from most people, surely from mine; and yet he is not at all a "bad" man.

AFTERWORD

1. Morris West, *The Shoes of the Fisherman* (New York: William Morrow, 1963), p. 270.
2. Pope Francis, *Evangelii Gaudium,* 97.
3. Pope Francis, *Evangelii Gaudium,* 120.

Breathing Under Water: Spirituality and the Twelve Steps

The Great Themes of Scripture: New Testament

The Great Themes of Scripture: Old Testament

*Hope Against Darkness: The Transforming Vision of Saint Francis
in an Age of Anxiety*

Jesus' Plan for a New World: The Sermon on the Mount

Preparing for Christmas: Daily Meditations for Advent

Silent Compassion: Finding God in Contemplation

Things Hidden: Scripture as Spirituality

Why Be Catholic?

Wild Man to Wise Man: Reflections on Male Spirituality

Wondrous Encounters: Scripture for Lent

Yes, And…: Daily Meditations

Center for
Action and
Contemplation

Home of THE ROHR INSTITUTE

Center for Action and Contemplation (CAC) is home to the Rohr Institute, an educational center grounded in the Christian mystical tradition. Founded by Richard Rohr, O.F.M., in 1987, CAC has a growing, international reach, touching lives regardless of denomination, religion or culture. CAC encourages the transformation of human consciousness through contemplation and seeks to equip and empower people to live out their sacred soul tasks in service to the world. Fr. Richard's teachings form the basis of the non-profit's vision and ongoing work.

CAC is located in Albuquerque, New Mexico, but many of its programs and resources can be accessed from anywhere in the world. Educational offerings include daily meditations (free emails sent every day), self-paced online courses, Living School (two-year program combining onsite and online learning), Conspire Symposia (annual events in New Mexico), online bookstore (comprehensive selection of Fr. Richard's books and recordings), and publications such as the journal *Oneing*.

Learn more at cac.org.